SUE DOLMAN'S
BOOK OF
ANIMAL
·TOYS·

Needleworkers and collectors, parents and children will be enchanted by all the well-loved and familiar animal characters featured in this book, and gifted toy designer Sue Dolman gives you the exciting opportunity to re-create this charming collection.

Whether your favourite is Freddie Fox, dressed as a poacher, pipe-smoking Bertie Badger in his best tweed suit or Kenny Koala, ready for the beach, you will be captivated by all the animal characters. The rest of the cast, in order of appearance, comprise Freda Fox, Brewster and Bertha Bear, Reggie and Rose Rabbit, and Mrs Maisie Mouse with her baby and two older children.

Each of the dozen projects includes actual-size patterns, clear, stage-by-stage instructional drawings to guide even the beginner through the construction processes, and detailed text descriptions of each step in making up the animals. The book also shows how clever use of clothing, and the addition of accessories for the finishing touches, can breathe life and personality into these little creatures. General guidance is also given on where to find suitable fabrics and trims.

Both the dedicated craft person and the less-experienced toymaker wishing to try a more challenging project can make and enjoy these adorable animals. As you follow the straightforward project guidelines, the full-colour photographs and Sue Dolman's exquisite artwork will inspire you to create your collection – and to pursue a satisfying and absorbing activity.

Sue Dolman is a professional toy designer and has created craft kits on a variety of subjects over several years, including a high-quality range of Kate Greenaway pot-faced dolls. She is also the author of the celebrated *Brambly Hedge Pattern Book*.

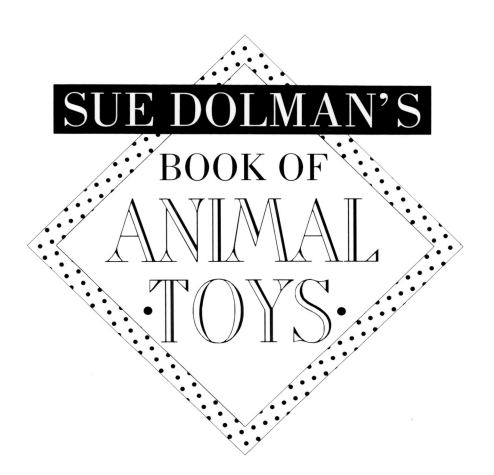

SUE DOLMAN'S

BOOK OF
ANIMAL
·TOYS·

CASSELL

Cassell
Wellington House
125 Strand
London WC2R 0BB

First published 1994
First paperback edition 1996

Distributed in the United States
by Sterling Publishing Co., Inc.
387 Park Avenue South, New York, New York 10016-8810

**British Library Cataloguing-in-Publication Data
A catalogue record for this book is available from
the British Library**

ISBN 0-304-34821-X

Typeset by Litho Link Limited, Welshpool, Powys

Printed in Hong Kong

Contents

·GENERAL INSTRUCTIONS·

1 FABRICS

Fabrics required for dressing the animals may already be close at hand. Your old cast-off jumpers, skirts and trousers may be perfect for making into tiny clothes. Charity shops and jumble sales are often places to find tweed in the form of men's suits. Cut out all usable parts and hand wash the pieces.

For small-patterned, printed cottons, look at dress fabrics or craft shops selling patchwork supplies. White cotton lace can be tinted cream by dipping it into black coffee. In the lists of materials, the origins of some items are given but quantities are not usually suggested, as they are less than the minimum amount that could be purchased.

2 FUR FABRIC

The choice of fur fabric is important. A short-pile, good-quality fur in an appropriate colour is essential if the animal is to look realistic. Try department stores and market stalls. To purchase fur, felt and bead eyes by mail order write to:

Candle House Crafts, Welham Road, Thorpe Langham, Leicestershire LE16 TU

3 EQUIPMENT

Sharp scissors Essential.
Sewing machine Useful, but pieces are small enough to stitch by hand.
Craft knife Cheap and disposable; used for cutting twigs. A blunt knife can be used for cutting thin wire; roll wire under the blade while pressing down onto thick card.
Long, thin darning needle For assembly of filled parts.
Paper for patterns Some writing papers are transparent enough for tracing.
Fine felt pen For drawing around patterns onto fabric.

4 PATTERNS

All patterns are printed full size and complete. Cover the page with paper. Trace carefully, following the inside of the printed line. This stops the patterns growing by the line thickness, which makes a difference to small pieces.

Mark eyes, nose and ears (if they are shown). Make pin holes in the pattern on these marks. Arrows on fur patterns indicate the direction of the fur pile. The fur trimming line need not be marked; this can be judged by eye later. Cut out paper patterns to the inside of the line.

5 CUTTING OUT THE FABRIC

Place patterns squarely on the wrong side of the fabric. Some of the collars are placed crossways to allow for stretching. Arrows on fur patterns follow the direction of the fur pile. Note whether a piece is cut out once, twice or turned over and cut again to make a pair. Lightly draw around patterns with a fine felt pen. Mark eye, ear and nose positions with the point of a pen pushed through pin holes in the pattern. Cut out fur in small snips using the points of the scissors; do not cut into the pile.

6 *TRIMMING THE FUR*

The pile on fur pieces is trimmed short in places to give shape to the head. Judge where the fine trim line on the pattern falls on the cut-out pieces. Lay scissors flat on the fur and trim pile evenly to half its length. Practise on scrap fur first. Graduate length over the trim line, leaving remainder long. Some ear pieces will be trimmed all over very short.

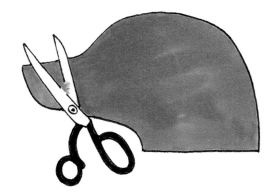

Mark nose and ears on the right side by taking a few stitches through the fur. Mark eyes with a tuft of threads. These can be removed after beads are stitched in place.

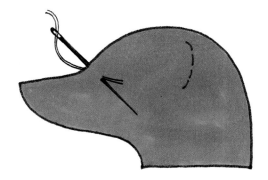

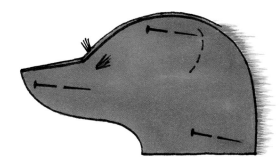

7 *STITCHING*

Match pieces with right sides together. Pin. A sewing machine can be used except on the fur and some of the felt pieces. These are oversewn on the edge with double thread.

Take small, close stitches and pull the thread tight to bite into the edge slightly. The second method is a small, straight running stitch. Stitch hems invisibly by just catching the right side of the fabric in the stitch.

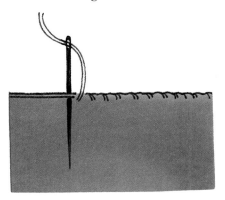

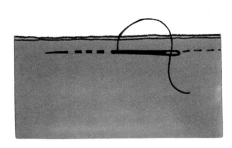

8 *TRIMMING THE SEAMS*

The edges of some seams need to be trimmed close to the stitching to reduce the bulk of the seam or clip into the seam if fraying could be a problem.

9 *TURNING TO RIGHT SIDE*

Use a flat-ended piece of wooden dowel to push into the stitched shapes without damaging the stitching. Never use a knitting needle. After turning, gently pull and ease the seams to smooth and flatten. Iron clothing pieces. Iron some ears through a cloth to make them as flat and thin as possible.

10 *FILLING*

Fill with small pinches at a time, gradually building up shape. Fill up to the openings. The flat-ended wooden dowel is good for easing in the filling.

11 *ASSEMBLY OF PARTS*

When they are first put on the body the finished trousers and bloomers look odd and badly fitting. Don't worry, they will be fine when they are filled, shaped and stitched to the body. Use the photographs of the animal as a guide while you work.

Stitch eyes into position using a long, thin darning needle. Go up through the gathers under the head to the eye position. Thread on the bead, then stitch back into the head and out through the gathers. Repeat with the other eye. Use strong thread and a long needle for stitching heads to bodies.

12 *GLUE*

Some tiny parts are better assembled with glue. Stand the tube in a cup and take off dots of glue with a pin. This stops glue going where you don't want it to.

SAFETY

The characters in the book are not suitable gifts for babies or young children because the eyes and small accessories can be easily removed.

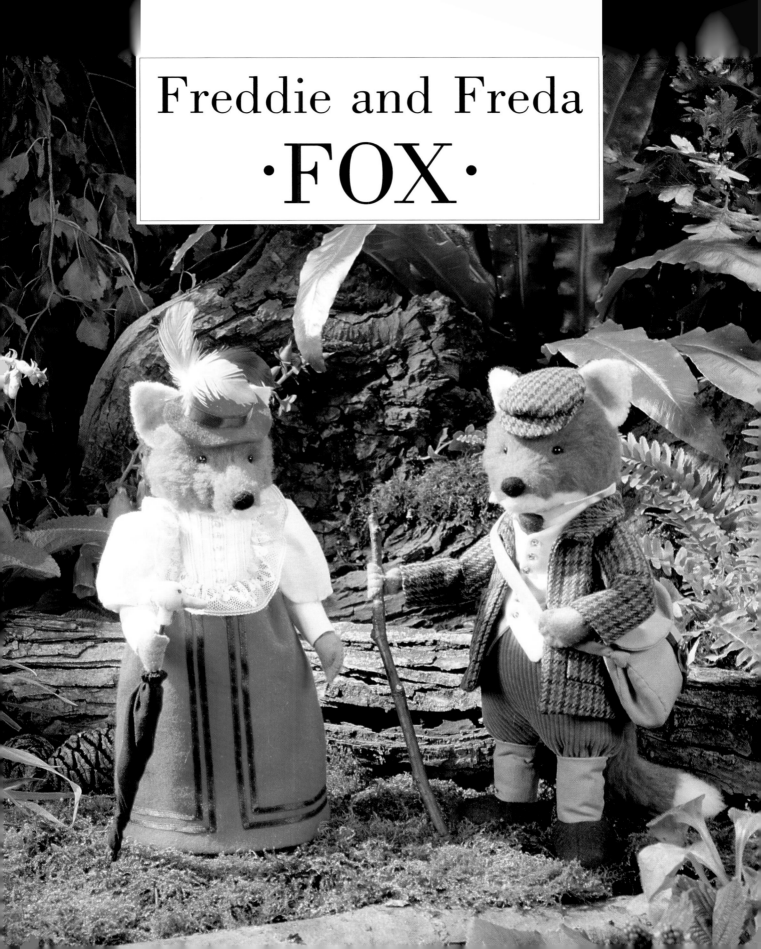

Freddie and Freda
·FOX·

Freddie FOX

Before starting work read General Instructions on pages 8, 9 and 10.

Materials

Head, ears and tail Tan, white and black fur, see General Instruction 2, page 8.

Eyes Black beads $\frac{5}{32}$ in (4 mm) in diameter.

Nose Black felt.

Hands and arms Tan felt to match fur.

Body and legs White felt.

Shoes and tie Dark brown felt. Stiff card.

Collar White cotton.

Waistcoat Cream cotton (curtain lining). Six small glass beads.

Trousers Corduroy (cut from an old jacket).

Jacket and cap Lightweight tweed (cut from an old skirt).

Bag and gaiters Pale brown cotton. Scrap of leather (cut from an old glove) Buckle ¾ in (19 mm) long (from a child's sandal or shoe repair shop). Feather (plucked from a duster).

Other Materials Polyester fibre toy filling. Strong thread. A twig. All-purpose clear adhesive. Threads to match felt.

Patterns

Trace and cut out, keeping to the inside of the line.

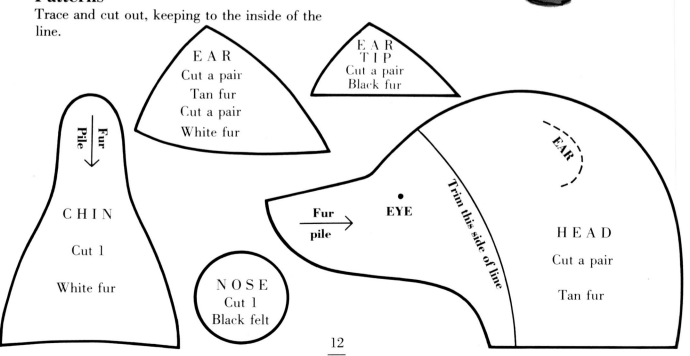

EAR
Cut a pair
Tan fur
Cut a pair
White fur

Fur Pile

EAR TIP
Cut a pair
Black fur

CHIN
Cut 1
White fur

NOSE
Cut 1
Black felt

Fur pile →

EYE

Trim this side of line

EAR

HEAD
Cut a pair
Tan fur

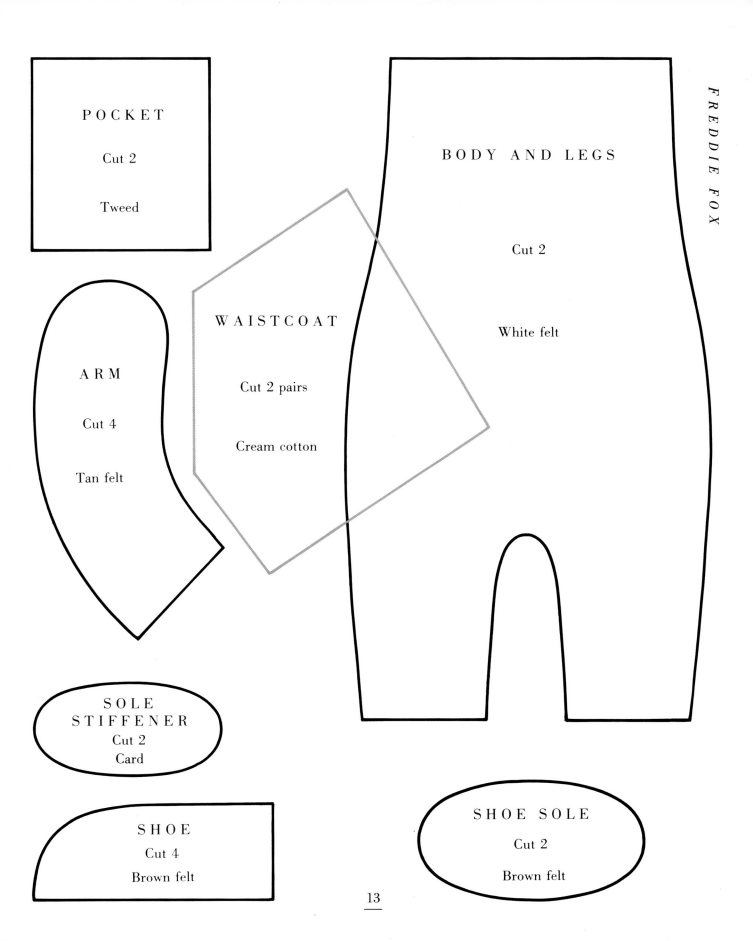

POCKET

Cut 2

Tweed

BODY AND LEGS

FREDDIE FOX

Cut 2

White felt

ARM

Cut 4

Tan felt

WAISTCOAT

Cut 2 pairs

Cream cotton

SOLE
STIFFENER
Cut 2
Card

SHOE

Cut 4

Brown felt

SHOE SOLE

Cut 2

Brown felt

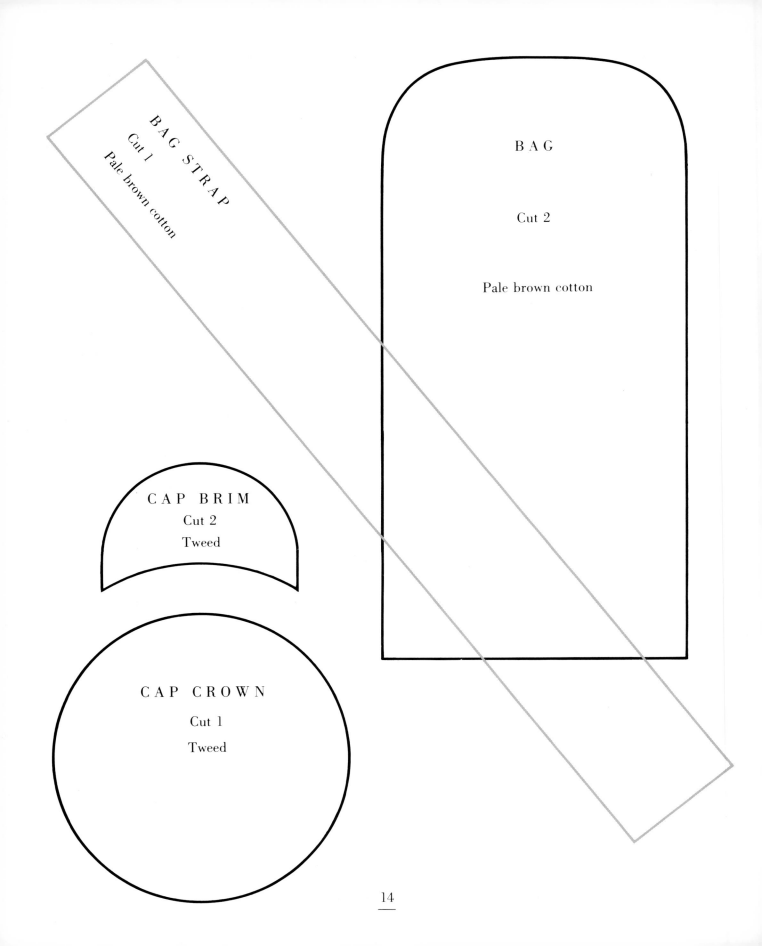

BAG STRAP

Cut 1

Pale brown cotton

BAG

Cut 2

Pale brown cotton

CAP BRIM

Cut 2

Tweed

CAP CROWN

Cut 1

Tweed

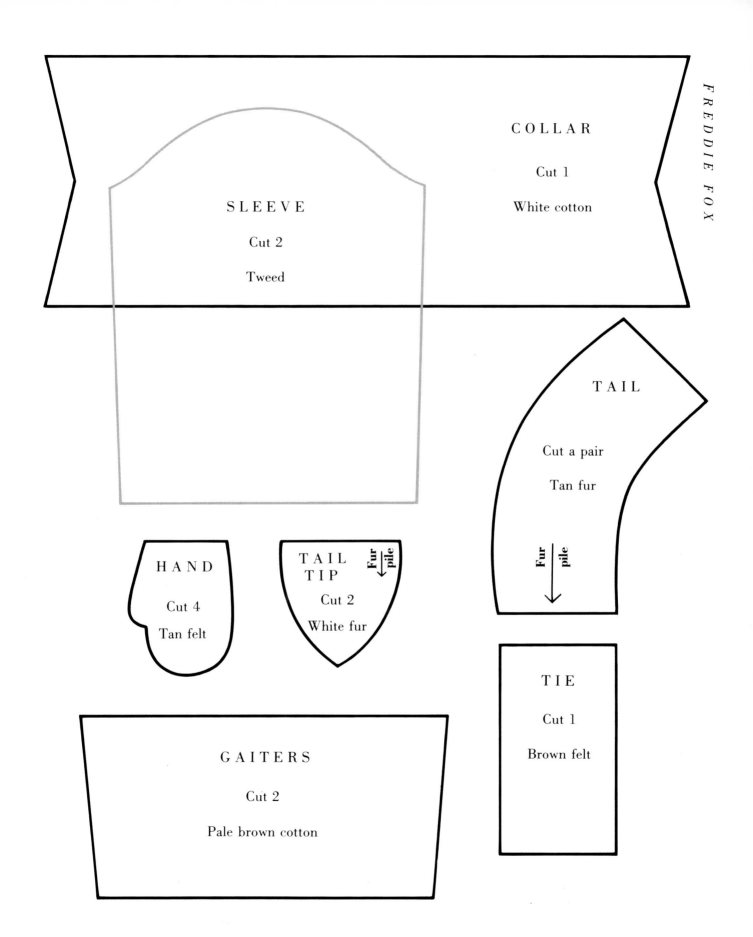

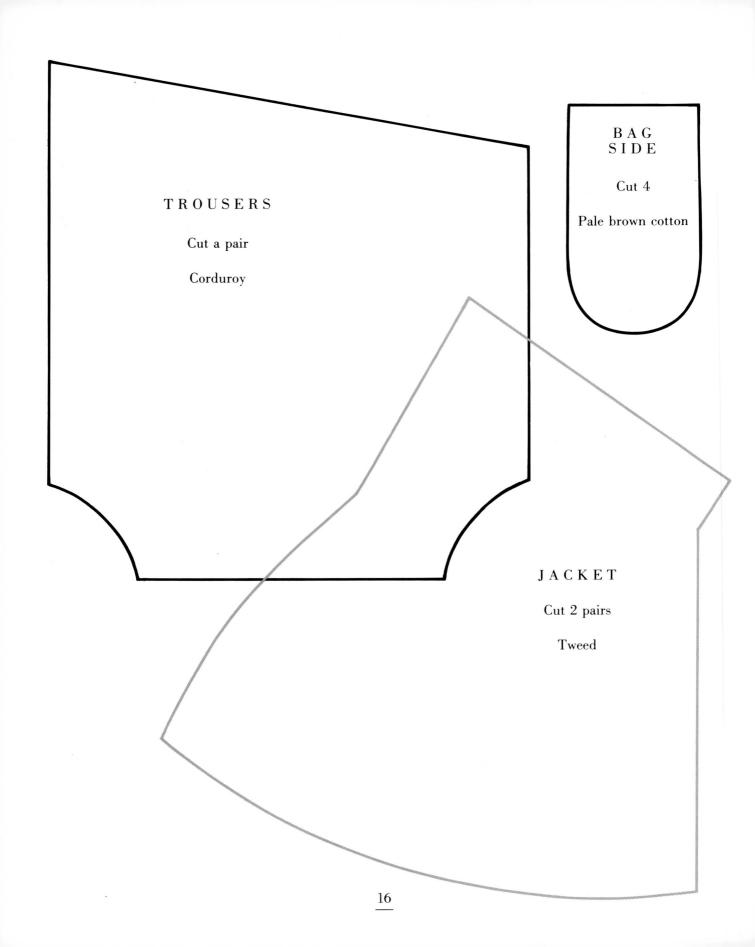

TROUSERS

Cut a pair

Corduroy

**B A G
S I D E**

Cut 4

Pale brown cotton

J A C K E T

Cut 2 pairs

Tweed

Freddie FOX

Instructions

HEAD

△ **1** Trim fur pile on head pieces as shown on pattern. See General Instruction 6, page 9. Mark eye and ear positions.

△ **2** Match head pieces. Oversew edge.

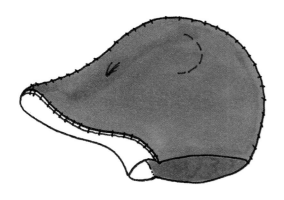

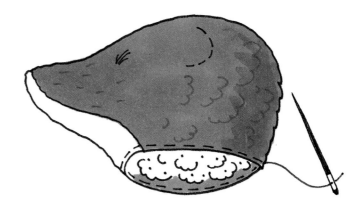

△ **3** Trim fur pile on chin piece all over. Match rounded end of chin centrally into head. Oversew edge.

△ **4** Turn to right side. Fill up to the opening, rounding the back well but keeping the nose slim and pointed. Gather on the edge. Pull up tight to close.

NOSE

◁ **5** Gather around the edge. Roll a pinch of filling into a ball, place in the centre. Pull up gathers very tight. Squash into an oval shape. Set aside until later.

 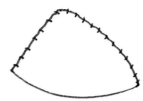 

EARS

△ **6** Trim fur pile short on all six pieces. Match the wrong side of one black tip to the right side of one tan piece. Stitch across the bottom edge of black tip.

△ **7** Match one white ear to tan/black ear with right sides together. Oversew edge. Turn to right side. Iron.

△ **8** Put a pin into the shortest edge of the ear. Oversew across bottom edges, pulling tight to curve the edge slightly.

◁ **9** Position ears on head as marked, with the pinned edges to the centre. Bottoms of ears should be ¾ in (19 mm) apart. Pin. Stitch. Stitch bead eyes over marks. Sit nose on tan fur, just touching the white fur. Pin. Stitch. From the nose measure 1 in (25 mm) under the chin. At this point take a stitch from side to side, looping the thread under the chin. Pull up slightly. Repeat a couple of times. Set head aside.

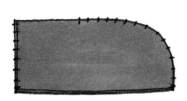 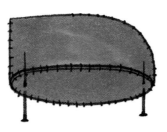 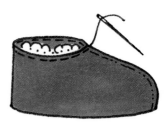

SHOES

△ **10** Match two side pieces. Oversew edge using tiny, close stitches pulled tight. Leave the bottom and 1 in (25 mm) of top open.

△ **11** Ease sole into shoe. Pin. Oversew edge. Turn to right side.

△ **12** Position card sole in shoe. Fill firmly up to the top. Gather around on the edge. Pull up tight. Set aside.

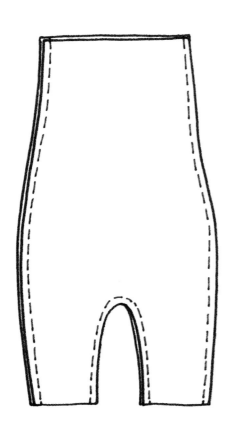

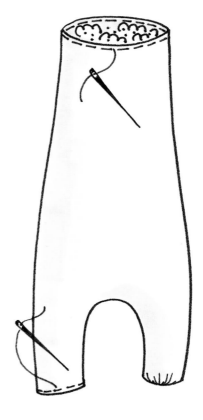

BODY AND LEGS

◁ **13** Match pieces. Stitch ¼ in (6 mm) from the edge. Trim away edges close to stitching. Turn to right side.

▷ **14** Fill firmly up to the openings. Take care not to stretch the felt upwards while filling. Gather around openings on the edge. Pull up gathers tight to close. Set aside.

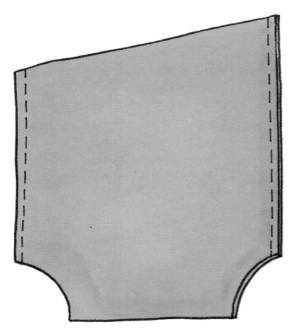

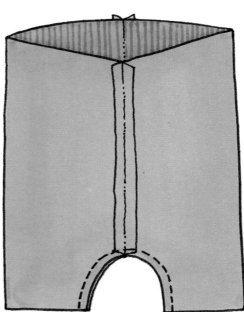

TROUSERS

△ **15** Match pieces. Stitch ¼ in (6 mm) from edge. Open and flatten seams.

△ **16** Fold to match inside legs. Stitch ¼ in (6 mm) from edge. Trim inside leg seam edges. Turn to right side.

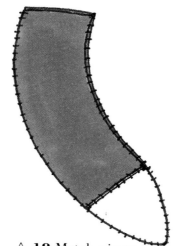

TAIL

△ **17** Match one white tip to one tail piece. Oversew edge. Repeat with other pieces.

△ **18** Match pieces. Oversew edge. Turn to right side. Gather around open end. Pull up tight. Set aside.

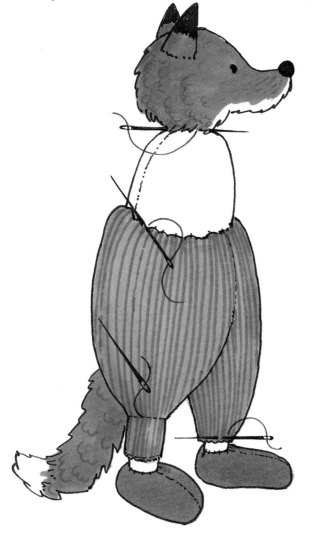

△ **19** Dress body in trousers, with high top at the back. Push trouser legs up out of the way. Pin. Press leg bottom over gathers on shoe top, with toes pointing slightly outwards. Pin. Stitch around twice, pulling together. Pull trousers well up. Slip small pinches of filling into trousers around leg tops and body, smoothly rounding tummy and bottom. Fill loosely with just enough to hold shape. Gather around top, ¼ in (6 mm) from the edge. Fold top inside on gather line. Pull up tight to fit.

◁ **20** Stitch trouser top to body. Pull trouser bottoms well down. Pin. Stitch bottom edge to leg. Gather around trouser leg 1 in (25 mm) up from the top of the shoe. Pull up to fit leg tightly. Position tail 2½ in (63 mm) down from trouser top. Stitch. Sit head on body. Beginning with large, loose stitches in the centre of both, pull head to body comfortably. Stitch between where they touch.

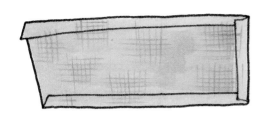

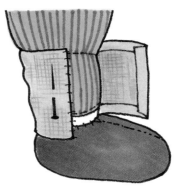

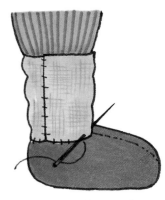

GAITERS

△ **21** Take one piece. Fold three edges ¼ in (6 mm) to wrong side. Iron.

△ **22** Beginning on the outside of the leg and touching the shoe top, wrap the gaiter around. Pin. Stitch.

△ **23** Wrap other end over, fitting well but leave slightly wrinkled. Pin. Stitch invisibly down edge and around shoe top.

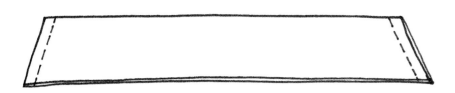

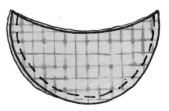

COLLAR

△ **24** Fold in half through the length. Stitch ¼ in (6 mm) from edge. Trim edges. Turn to right side. Iron. Set aside.

CAP BRIM

△ **25** Match pieces. Stitch ¼ in (6 mm) from edge. Trim edge. Turn to right side. Iron.

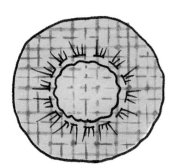

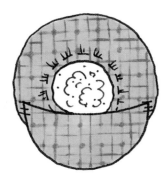

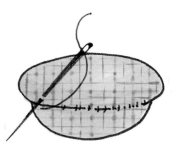

CAP CROWN

△ **26** Gather around the edge. Pull up to measure 1¾ in (45 mm) across the whole cap.

△ **27** Position brim so that it protrudes ¼ in (6 mm) forwards under crown. Stitch corners. Push tiny pinches of filling into crown around edges.

△ **28** Stitch across where brim and crown touch. Set aside.

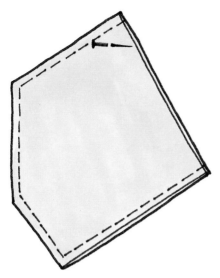

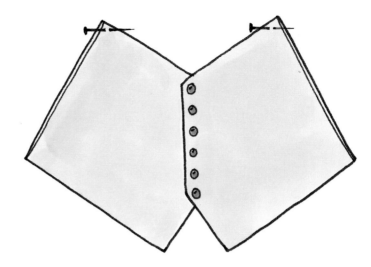

WAISTCOAT

△ **29** To save confusion, pin top corners after cutting out. Match one pair. Stitch ¼ in (6 mm) from edge. Trim edges. Turn to right side. Iron. Repeat with other pair.

△ **30** Match pieces, with centre fronts overlapping by ¼ in (6 mm). Pin. Stitch beads to centre front, taking stitches through both waistcoat pieces to hold together.

TIE

△ **31** Fold long edges to touch. Iron.

△ **32** Fold in half. Wrap thread around twice, pulling tight. Fasten off thread. Set aside.

▷ **33** Sit cap on head. Pin. Stitch through cap into head. Wrap collar around neck, so it stands up high. Where corners meet under the chin, stitch between and into body. Glue tie over collar under chin. Dress waistcoat high onto chest, fitting it closely. Pin. Stitch side edges to body.

JACKET

▷ **34** Match one pair. Stitch ¼ in (6 mm) from edge, leaving the bottom 1½ in (38 mm) unstitched. Open out flat, including the seam. Iron through a cloth. Repeat with other pair.

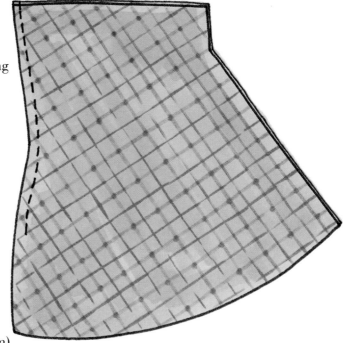

▽ **35** Match pieces. Stitch around ¼ in (6 mm) from edge. Trim edges and corners. Turn to right side through the centre back opening. Carefully poke out corners and seams to their fullest. Iron through a damp cloth.

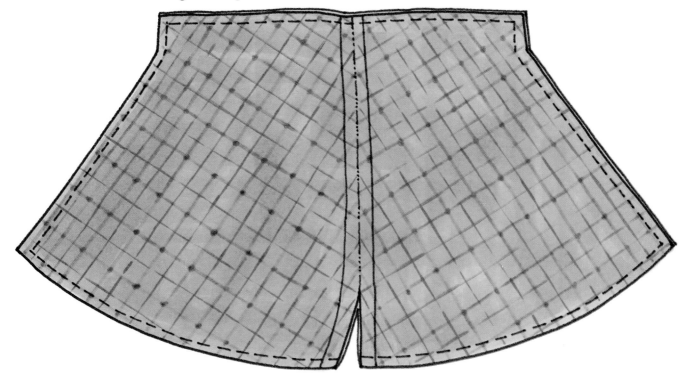

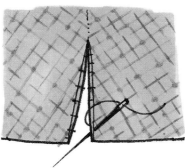

△ **36** Match folded edges of the centre back opening to form a vent. Oversew edge.

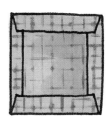

POCKETS

△ **37** Take one piece. Fold all edges to wrong side by ¼ in (6 mm). Iron. Position on jacket front ½ in (13 mm) from both edges. Pin. Stitch. Repeat with other pocket. Set jacket aside.

HANDS

△ **38** Match two pieces. Oversew on edge with tiny, tight stitches in the same colour thread as felt.

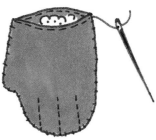

△ **39** Stitch three equal lines through both layers of felt. Fill palm. Gather around on the edge. Pull up tight. Set aside.

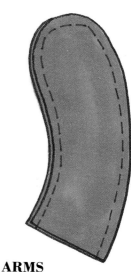

ARMS

△ **40** Match two pieces. Stitch ¼ in (6 mm) from edge. Trim edge. Turn to right side.

◁ **41** Fill loosely. Gather around bottom on the edge. Pull up tight.

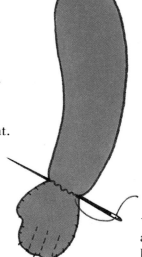

◁ **42** Butt hand to arm. Pin. Stitch between.

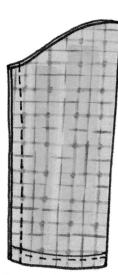

SLEEVE

△ **43** Fold up bottom edge by ¼ in (6 mm). Stitch. Fold sleeve with right sides together. Stitch ¼ in (6 mm) from edge. Turn to right side.

△ **44** Push arm into sleeve. Pin. Gather sleeve top close to edge. Pull up tight, tucking edges inside. Stitch through gathers into arm. Set aside.

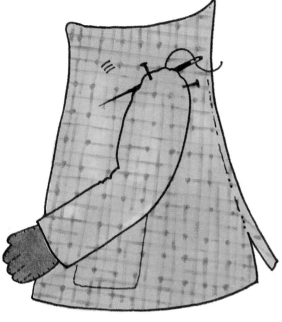

△ **45** Fold jacket collar ½ in (13 mm) over to right side. Iron. Wrap jacket around fox, with collar high at the back. Pin to fox's body at front. Slip a long needle from side to side under the jacket collar and going through the body. Assess positions for the sleeve tops. Take a couple of stitches through the jacket and into the body at this point.

◁ **46** Position sleeve on the jacket side. Pin. Take stitches between jacket and the inner side of sleeve top, where they meet comfortably.

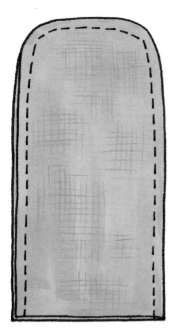

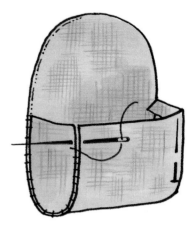

48 Repeat step 47 for the bag sides, making both exactly as the larger piece.

49 Match sides into bag, butting edges together. Pin. Oversew, just catching edges.

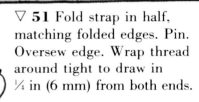

BAG

△ **47** Match pieces. Stitch ¼ in (6 mm) from edge. Trim edge. Turn to right side. Iron. Take edges of the open end and, both together, fold over by ¼ in (6 mm). Iron.

△ **50** Fold short edges of bag strap to wrong side. Iron. Fold both long edges to wrong side by ¼ in (6 mm). Iron.

▽ **51** Fold strap in half, matching folded edges. Pin. Oversew edge. Wrap thread around tight to draw in ¼ in (6 mm) from both ends.

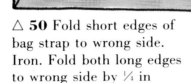

◁ **52** Pinch the top corners of bag side together. Stitch. Position end of strap over stitches. Stitch. Repeat with other side. Cut a piece of soft leather ¼ in (6 mm) x 2 in (50 mm). Cut one end to a point. Make a hole in the centre of the leather with a thick needle. Thread on the buckle. Glue strap centrally on bag. Fill bag softly. Bring flap down and glue to hold. Glue a feather into the corner. Lay bag strap over fox's shoulder. Stitch hand to strap in a natural position.

▷ **53** Wrap other hand around a stick. Stitch between finger ends and hand.

Freda FOX

Before starting work read General
Instructions on pages 8, 9 and 10.

Materials

Head, ears and tail Tan, white and black fur; see
General Instruction 2, page 8.

Eyes Black beads ⁵⁄₃₂ in (4 mm) in diameter.

Nose Black felt.

Hands and arms Tan felt to match fur.

Body and legs White felt.

Shoes Dark brown felt. Stiff card.

Hat Red felt. Brown satin ribbon ¼ in (6 mm)
wide. Feathers (plucked from a duster).

Umbrella Pale and bright yellow felt. Black cotton
fabric. Wooden dowel ⅛ in (3 mm) in diameter (from
woodwork shop) or wooden skewer (from kitchen shop).
Black felt pen. Black embroidery thread.

Bloomers White cotton. Lace ½ in (13 mm) wide.

Blouse Cream cotton. Cream lace 1 in (25 mm)
wide, 39 in (1 m) long (use the type of lace that
has only one straight edge). Smallest pearl beads.

Skirt Flannel, brushed cotton or winceyette. Brown
satin ribbon ⅛ in (3 mm) wide, 58 in (1.5 m) long.

Other materials Polyester fibre toy filling. All-purpose
clear adhesive. Strong thread. Threads to match felt.

Patterns

Trace and cut out, keeping to the inside of
the line.

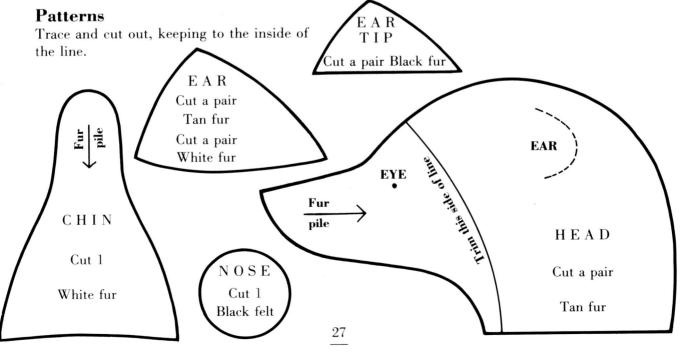

CHIN

Cut 1

White fur

Fur pile ↓

EAR

Cut a pair
Tan fur

Cut a pair
White fur

EAR TIP

Cut a pair Black fur

NOSE

Cut 1
Black felt

Fur pile →

EYE

Trim this side of line

EAR

HEAD

Cut a pair

Tan fur

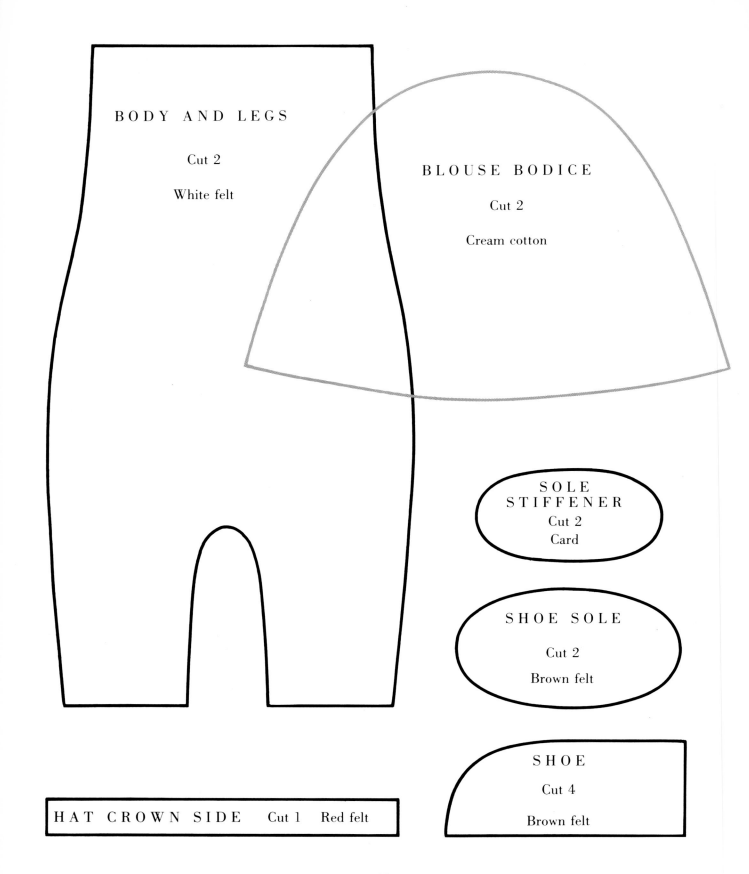

BODY AND LEGS

Cut 2

White felt

BLOUSE BODICE

Cut 2

Cream cotton

SOLE
STIFFENER
Cut 2
Card

SHOE SOLE

Cut 2

Brown felt

SHOE

Cut 4

Brown felt

HAT CROWN SIDE   Cut 1   Red felt

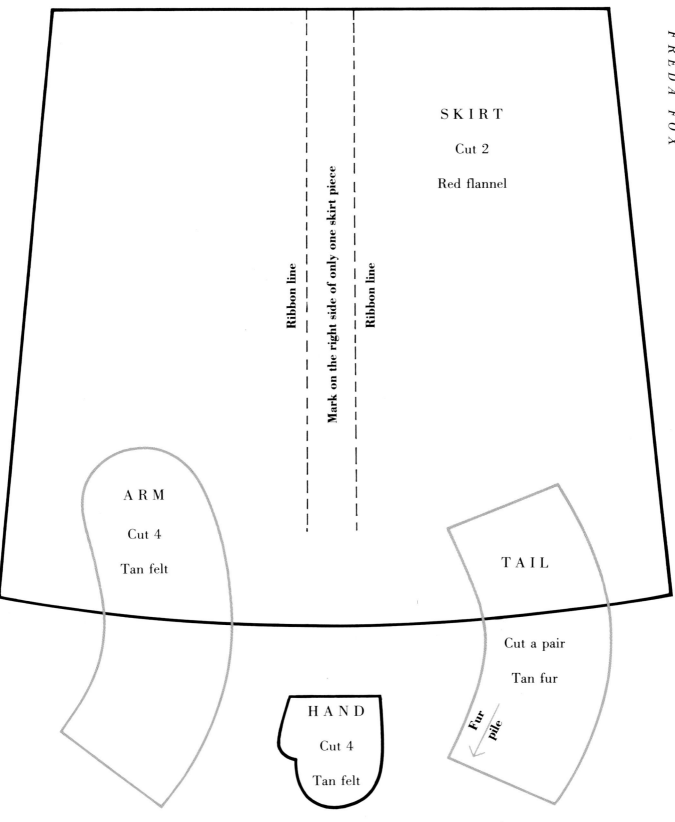

S K I R T

Cut 2

Red flannel

Ribbon line

Mark on the right side of only one skirt piece

Ribbon line

A R M

Cut 4

Tan felt

T A I L

Cut a pair

Tan fur

Fur pile

H A N D

Cut 4

Tan felt

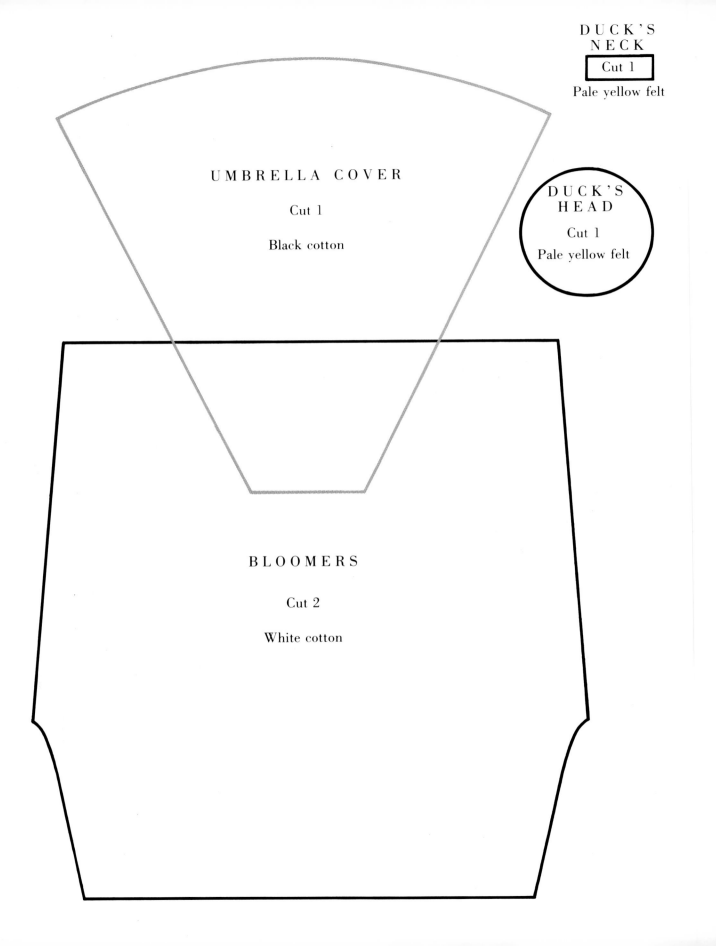

DUCK'S
NECK

Cut 1

Pale yellow felt

DUCK'S
HEAD

Cut 1
Pale yellow felt

UMBRELLA COVER

Cut 1

Black cotton

BLOOMERS

Cut 2

White cotton

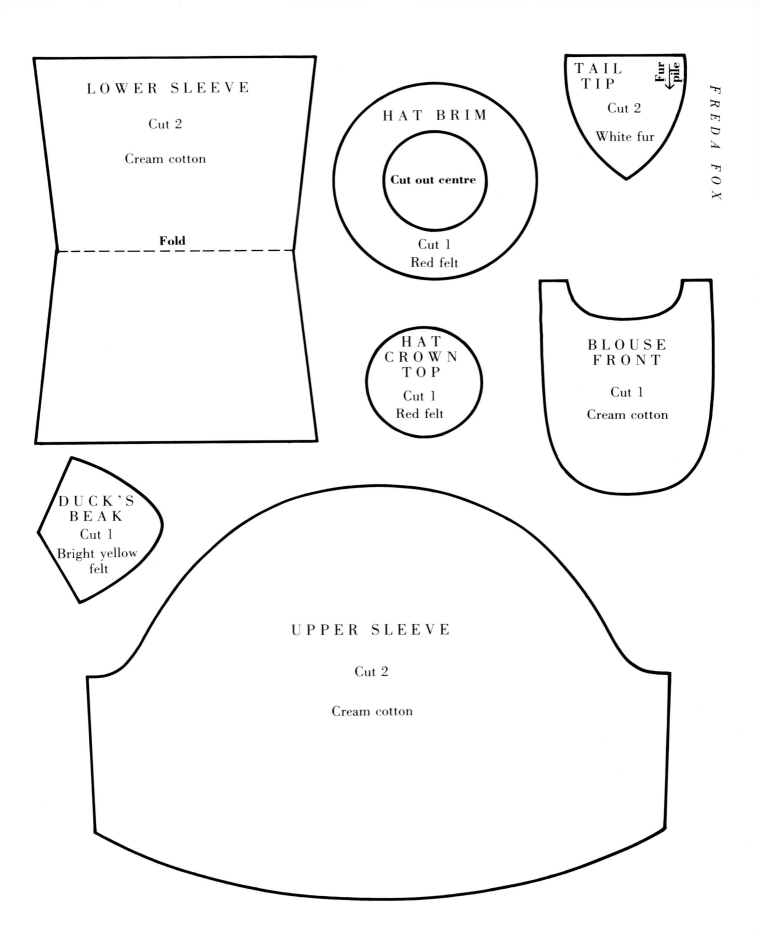

Freda FOX

Instructions

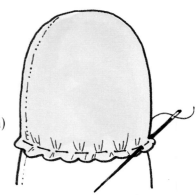

HEAD, NOSE, EARS, SHOES, BODY AND LEGS

1 See instructions for Freddie Fox, steps 1–14, pages 17–19.

BLOUSE BODICE

◁ **2** Match pieces. Stitch ¼ in (6 mm) from edge. Trim edges close to stitching. Turn to right side.

▷ **3** Gather around bottom on the edge. Pull bodice over body, with side seams of both matching. Pull up gathers to fit. The whole bodice will be slightly loose. Stitch through gathers into body.

BLOOMERS

◁ **4** Take one piece. Fold up bottom edge by ¼ in (6 mm). Stitch. Place lace overhanging bottom edge. Gather and stitch to edge at the same time. Repeat with other piece.

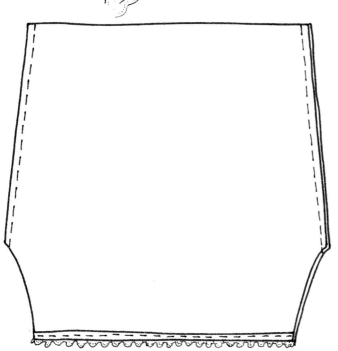

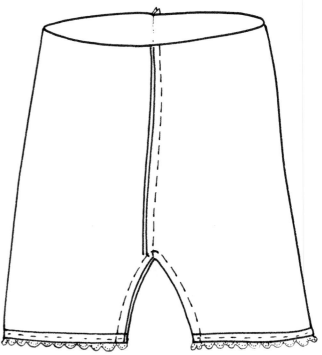

△ **5** Match pieces. Stitch ¼ in (6 mm) from edge.

△ **6** Fold to match inside legs. Stitch ¼ in (6 mm) from edge. Trim inside leg seam close to stitching. Turn to right side.

▷ **7** Dress body in bloomers. Push bloomer legs up out of the way. Pin. Press leg bottom over gathers on shoe top, with toes pointing slightly outwards. Pin. Stitch around twice, pulling together. Pull bloomers well up. Slip small pinches of filling into the bloomers at the back to round the bottom. Gather around top ¼ in (6 mm) from the edge. Fold inside on the gather line. Pull up tight to fit. Stitch top of bloomers to body. Sit head on body. Beginning with large, loose stitches in the centre of both, pull head to body comfortably. Stitch between where they touch.

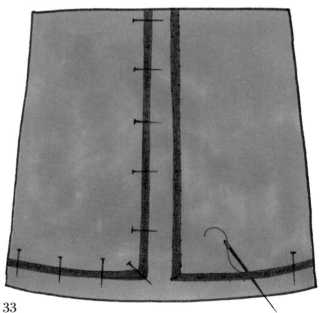

TAIL

8 See instructions for Freddie Fox, steps 17 and 18, page 20. Position tail 2½ in (63 mm) down from top of bloomers. Stitch.

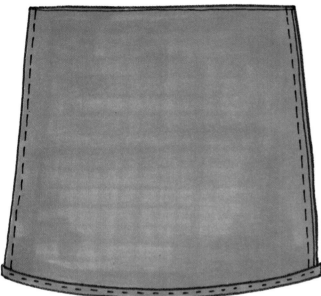

SKIRT

△ **9** Take one piece. Mark ribbon lines on the right side with a sharp pencil and ruler. Match pieces. Stitch ¼ in (6 mm) from the edge. Fold up bottom edge ¼ in (6 mm). Stitch. Turn to right side. Iron.

▷ **10** Match edge of ⅛ in (3 mm) wide ribbon to the outside of one pencil line, beginning at the skirt top. Use lots of pins, placing them over the ribbon, not through it. Turn ribbon at right angles ¾ in (19 mm) from the bottom. Pin. Continue placing ribbon parallel to the skirt bottom. Pin. Arriving back at the centre front, turn at right angles to match edge to the outside of the other pencil line. Pin. Stitch ribbon to skirt, just catching the edge.

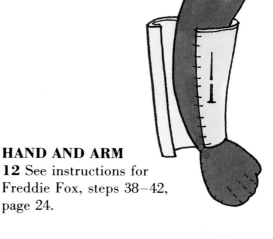

HAND AND ARM
12 See instructions for Freddie Fox, steps 38–42, page 24.

LOWER SLEEVE
△ **13** Take one piece and fold in half. Wrap sleeve around arm with fold at the wrist. Pin. Stitch to arm.

△ **11** No need for a pencil line this time. Repeat with next ribbon, beginning on the outside of the first downward ribbon and keeping exactly ⅛ in (3 mm) apart all round. Pin, stitch and iron. Gather around skirt top ¼ in (6 mm) from the edge. Set skirt aside.

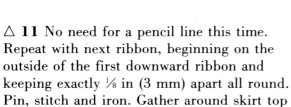

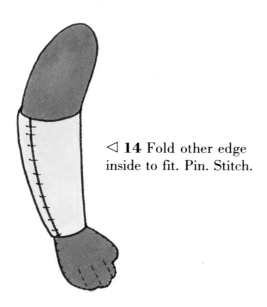

◁ **14** Fold other edge inside to fit. Pin. Stitch.

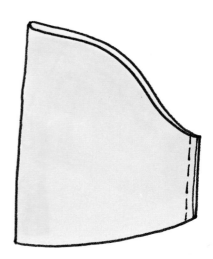

△ UPPER SLEEVE
15 Take one piece. Fold to match edges. Stitch ¼ in (6 mm) from edge. Turn to right side.

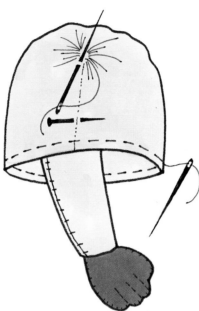

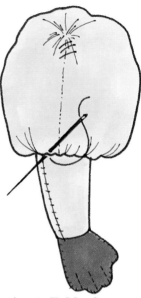

△ **16** Gather around ¼ in (6 mm) from edge. Pull up tight, tucking edges inside.

▷ **17** Pop arm into upper sleeve so that top ½ in (13 mm) of arm is against gathers on sleeve top. Pin. Stitch. Gather ¼ in (6 mm) from the bottom edge. Slip a small fluffed out pinch of filling between the outer side of arm and upper sleeve.

△ **18** Fold edge inside on gathers. Pull gathers up tight to fit over the top of the lower sleeve. Stitch between upper and lower sleeves.

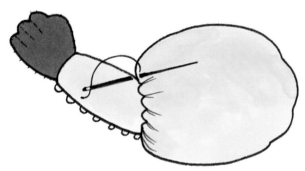

△ **19** Stitch pearl beads along lower sleeve. Bend arm. Pin. Hold with a couple of stitches.

▷ **20** Dress body in skirt. Fold top inside on gather line. Pull up tight, pressing well down over bloomers. Stitch through skirt top into body. Hold the fullness of the sleeve away from the arm top with a pin. Position sleeve on side of body ½ in (13 mm) down from the head. Pin. Take stitches between body and inner side of the sleeve top where they touch comfortably.

HAT CROWN SIDE

△ **21** Butt short edges. Stitch between.

△ **22** Balance crown top on the sides. Oversew edge. Do not pull stitches too tight. Turn upside down.

△ **23** Lay brim over crown. Oversew edge. Lay ribbon around crown. Trim to fit. Glue ends at back. Glue feather ends between hat and ribbon.

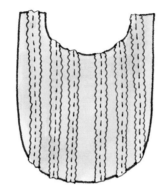

◁ **25** Lay the narrow edge of lace onto the blouse front in six equally spaced strips. Pin. Stitch.

BLOUSE FRONT

△ **24** Cut a 13 in (330 mm) length of lace. Cut away the narrow straight edge.

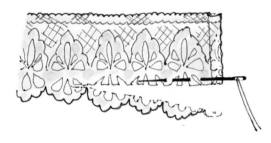

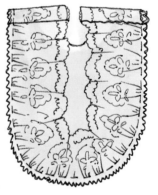

△ **26** Cut a 12 in (305 mm) length of lace. Cut away shaped edge to leave it ⅞ in (22 mm) wide. Fold short ends over. Gather across the cut edge, on the edge. Pull up to measure 5½ in (139 mm).

△ **27** Spread gathers evenly. Match gathers to the right side of blouse front. Pin. Stitch ⅛ in (3 mm) from edge, pulling stitches tight. Fold lace outwards. Iron through a cloth. Stitch seven pearl beads down the centre.

◁ **28** Position blouse front on body, with neckline high under chin. Pin. Stitch top corners to shoulders. Stitch invisibly from side to side, taking needle through the blouse bodice. Sit hat on top of head. Pin. Take needle side to side, through hat and head. Four stitches will do. Don't pull stitches too tight or you will distort the hat shape.

▷ **29** Cut a 6 in (150 mm) length of lace. Trim and gather in the same way as the last piece of lace for the blouse front. Pull up to fit across the back of the neck. Pin. Stitch ends to the ends of the lace around the blouse front and gathered edge to blouse around back of neck.

UMBRELLA

30 Take a 5½ in (139 mm) length of wooden dowel. Sharpen one end to a point. Colour with black felt pen. Allow to dry.

DUCK'S HEAD

△ **31** Gather around the edge with strong thread. Fill centre with enough stuffing to make a really hard shape. The gathers should be tough to pull up tight. If not, fill more. Pull up gathers halfway. Fasten off thread.

◁ **32** Push in stick. Gather around again over previous gathers. Pull up tight around stick. Fasten off thread. Remove stick, glue end and push back into head again.

▷ **33** Wrap neck around stick. Trim to fit. Glue into place.

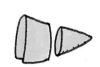

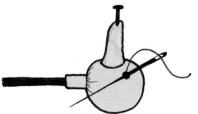

BEAK

△ **34** Fold in half. Oversew edge with tiny, tight stitches, stopping ½ in (13 mm) from the end. Turn to right side. Carefully pull out the point.

△ **35** Cut off wide end where stitches finish.

△ **36** Balance beak on the head. Pin. Stitch to head, just catching the edges. Squeeze beak flat. Make tiny spots for eyes with close stitches in black thread. Stitch between eyes. Pull together slightly.

COVER

▽ **37** Fold up bottom by ¼ in (6 mm). Iron. Fold in half. Stitch ¼ in (6 mm) from edge. Turn to right side.

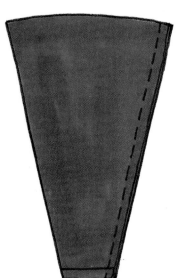

△ **38** Fold top of cover ½ in (13 mm) to wrong side. Gather through double fabric ¼ in (6 mm) down from the fold. Push stick into the cover. Put a spot of glue inside the cover at the bottom to hold the stick. Stitch outside to tighten. Pull up top gathers tight. Wrap thread twice round over the gathers. Pull tight.

△ **39** Curl hand around stick. Stitch across fingers into hand. Twist cover.

Brewster and Bertha
·BEAR·

Brewster BEAR

Before starting work read General Instructions on pages 8, 9 and 10.

Materials

Head and ears Brown fur; see General Instruction 2, page 8.

Eyes Black beads $5/32$ in (4 mm) in diameter.

Nose and shoes Black felt. Stiff card.

Hands and arms Brown felt to match fur.

Body and legs White felt.

Shirt White cotton.

Waistcoat Cream cotton (curtain lining). Smallest pearl beads.

Necktie Brown satin ribbon ½ in (13 mm) wide.

Trousers Black, white and grey check tweed (cut from a pair of lightweight trousers).

Coat Fine cotton velvet, fine needlecord or a fine plain woven wool.

Watch chain Gold chain (very cheap necklace bought from a market stall).

Other materials Polyester fibre toy filling. Strong thread. All-purpose clear adhesive. Threads to match felt.

Patterns

Trace and cut out, keeping to the inside of the line.

NOSE
Cut 1
Black felt

EAR
Cut 4
Brown fur

Fur pile →

Trim this side of line

HEAD SIDE

Cut a pair

Brown fur

Fur pile

EYES

Trim this side of line

EAR

EAR

HEAD CENTRE

Cut 1

Brown fur

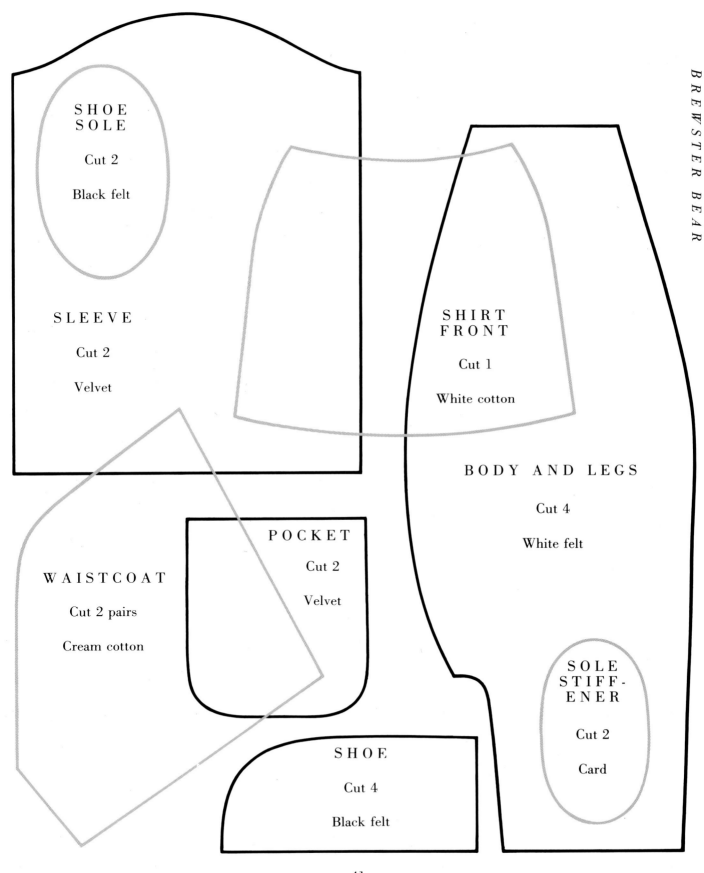

SHOE
SOLE

Cut 2

Black felt

SLEEVE

Cut 2

Velvet

SHIRT
FRONT

Cut 1

White cotton

BODY AND LEGS

Cut 4

White felt

WAISTCOAT

Cut 2 pairs

Cream cotton

POCKET

Cut 2

Velvet

SOLE
STIFF-
ENER

Cut 2

Card

SHOE

Cut 4

Black felt

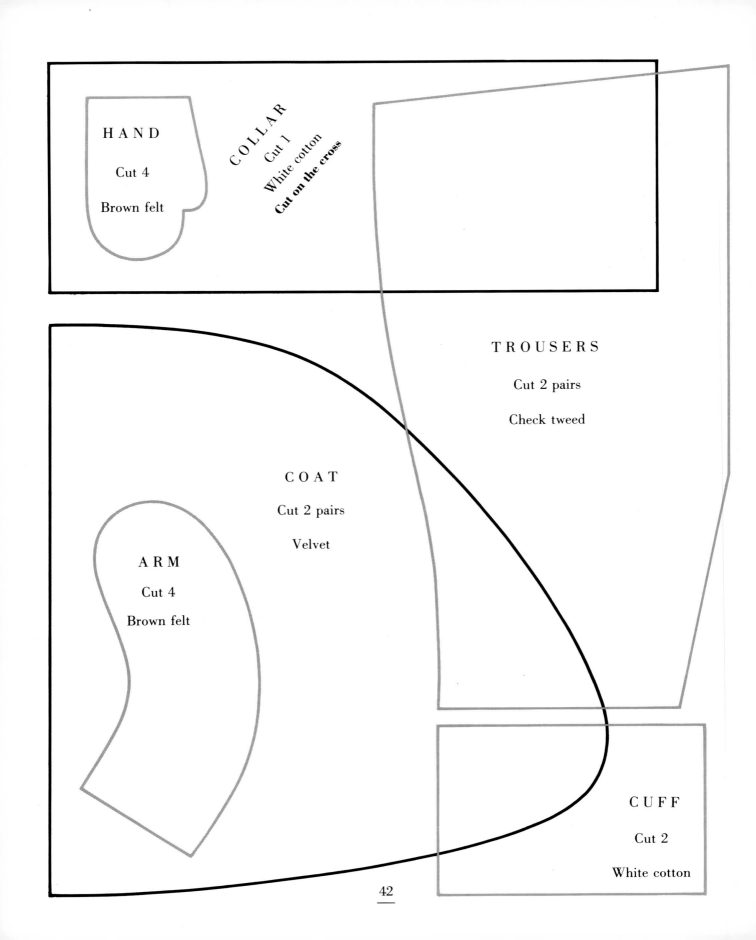

HAND

Cut 4

Brown felt

COLLAR

Cut 1

White cotton

Cut on the cross

TROUSERS

Cut 2 pairs

Check tweed

COAT

Cut 2 pairs

Velvet

ARM

Cut 4

Brown felt

CUFF

Cut 2

White cotton

Brewster BEAR
Instructions

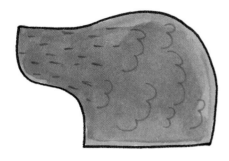
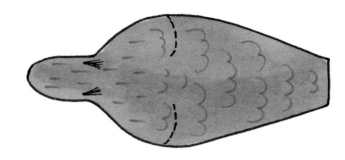

HEAD

△ **1** Trim fur pile on all head pieces as shown on pattern. Mark eye and ear positions.

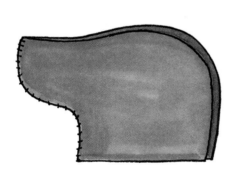

△ **2** Match head side pieces. Oversew edge.

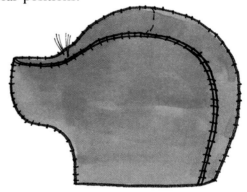

△ **3** Match rounded end of head centre piece, centrally into head. Oversew edge. Turn to right side.

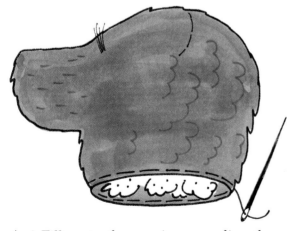

△ **4** Fill up to the opening, rounding the back and sides well. Gather on the edge. Pull up tight to close.

NOSE

△ **5** Fold over top edge by ⅛ in (3 mm). Stitch. Gather around curve on the very edge.

△ **6** Pull gathers up tight. Stitch side to side through the edge of gathers pulling tight. Set aside.

EARS

△ **7** Trim fur pile short on all pieces. Match two pieces. Oversew edge. Turn to right side.

△ **8** Oversew across bottom, pulling tight to curve the edge slightly.

▷ **9** Position ears as marked. Bottoms of ears should be 1¼ in (32 mm) apart. Pin. Stitch. Stitch bead eyes over marks. Position nose with gathers at the bottom. Stitch to face just catching the nose edges. Take a stitch from side to side, looping under the chin against the head. Pull up slightly. Repeat a couple of times. Set head aside.

SHOES

10 See instructions for Freddie Fox, steps 10–12, page 18.

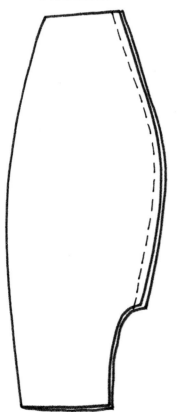

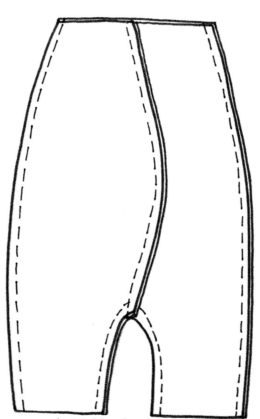

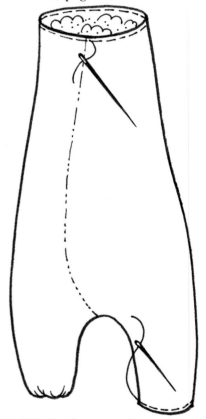

BODY AND LEGS

△ **11** Match two pieces. Stitch ¼ in (6 mm) from the edge. Open out flat. Repeat with other two pieces.

△ **12** Match pieces. Stitch ¼ in (6 mm) from the edge. Trim edges close to stitching. Turn to right side.

△ **13** Fill firmly up to the openings. Take care not to stretch the felt upwards while filling. Gather around openings on the edge. Pull up tight to close. Set aside.

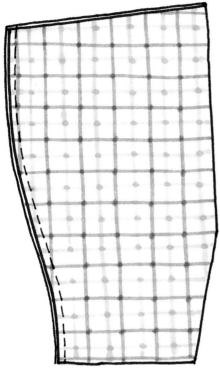

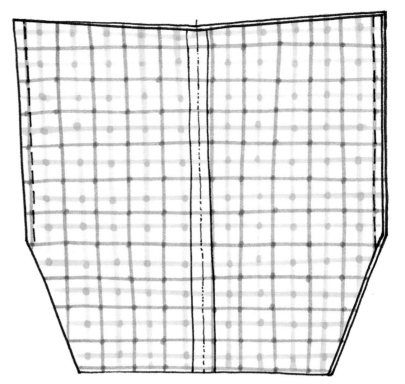

TROUSERS

△ **14** Match one pair. Stitch ¼ in (6 mm) from edge. Open out pieces and flatten seams. Iron through a cloth. Repeat with other pair.

△ **15** Match pieces. Stitch ¼ in (6 mm) from edge. Open out and flatten seams. Iron.

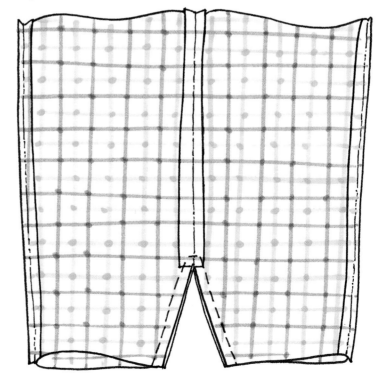

▷ **16** Fold to match inside legs. Stitch ¼ in (6 mm) from edge. Trim inside leg seam edges. Turn to right side.

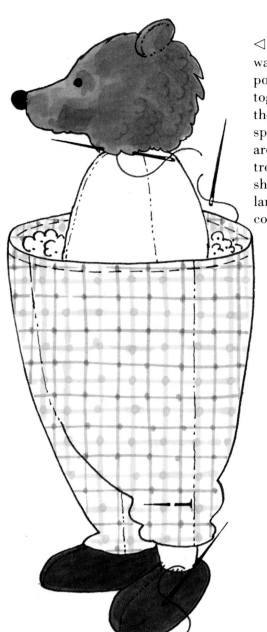

◁ **17** Dress body in trousers. Push trouser legs up out of way. Pin. Press leg bottom over gathers on shoe top, with toes pointing slightly outwards. Pin. Stitch around twice, pulling together. Pull trousers well up. Fill the trouser back to round the bear's bottom. Fill the trouser front more than the back, spreading the filling smoothly to the sides and top. Gather around top. Pull up to fit. Stitch through top into body. Fold trouser leg bottoms inside. Stitch through folded edge into shoe top at the side seams. Sit head on body. Beginning with large, loose stitches in the centre of both, pull head to body comfortably. Stitch between where they touch.

SHIRT FRONT

▷ **18** Position on chest, high under chin. Pin side edges, leaving front loose enough to slide in some filling. Stitch side edges to body. Smoothly fill under shirt front. Stitch across bottom into trousers.

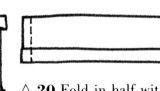

COLLAR

△ **19** Fold long edges ¼ in (6 mm) to wrong side. Iron.

△ **20** Fold in half with right sides together. Stitch ¼ in (6 mm) from edges. Trim edges and corners. Turn to right side. Iron. Wrap collar around neck. Stitch across front and into body.

46

NECKTIE

△ **21** Cut a ribbon 6½ in (165 mm) long. Fold in half through the length. Iron. Wrap around neck over the collar. Stitch ends at back. To make bow, cut two ribbons 3½ in (89 mm) long. Fold each one and thread onto a needle, stitch through centres.

△ **22** Wrap thread tightly around centre a few times, glue bow over centre front.

WAISTCOAT

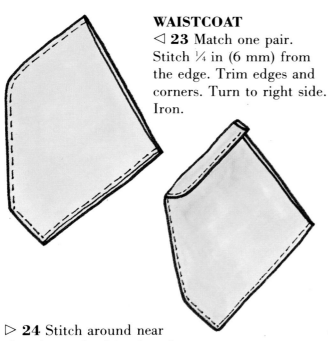

◁ **23** Match one pair. Stitch ¼ in (6 mm) from the edge. Trim edges and corners. Turn to right side. Iron.

▷ **24** Stitch around near the edge with white thread for decoration. Fold the top ⅜ in (10 mm) over to right side to make a collar. Iron. Repeat with other piece.

△ **25** Lay waistcoat pieces over bear's tummy with centres just overlapping and top corners over the necktie band. Pin. Slip unseen stitches under the centre fronts to hold together. Stitch side edges to body. Stitch pearl beads down the front. Cut a 4 in (100 mm) length of chain. Stitch chain in three places to waistcoat.

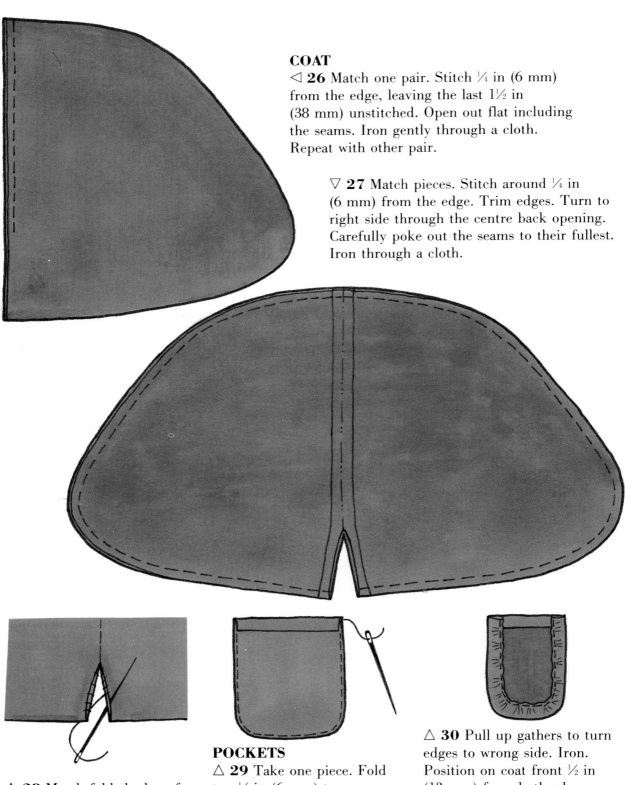

COAT

◁ **26** Match one pair. Stitch ¼ in (6 mm) from the edge, leaving the last 1½ in (38 mm) unstitched. Open out flat including the seams. Iron gently through a cloth. Repeat with other pair.

▽ **27** Match pieces. Stitch around ¼ in (6 mm) from the edge. Trim edges. Turn to right side through the centre back opening. Carefully poke out the seams to their fullest. Iron through a cloth.

△ **28** Match folded edge of the centre back opening to form a vent. Oversew edge.

POCKETS

△ **29** Take one piece. Fold top ¼ in (6 mm) to wrong side. Iron. Gather around on the edge.

△ **30** Pull up gathers to turn edges to wrong side. Iron. Position on coat front ½ in (13 mm) from both edges. Pin. Stitch. Repeat with other pocket. Set coat aside.

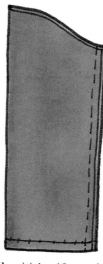

HANDS AND ARMS
31 See instructions for Freddie Fox, steps 38 – 42, page 24.

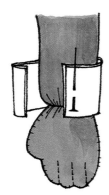

CUFFS
◁ **32** Take one piece. Fold in half through the length. Iron. Wrap around wrist with 1⅛ in (29 mm) of hand showing. Pin.

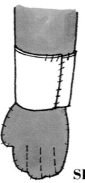

◁ **33** Wrap other end over, folding edge inside to fit. Stitch.

SLEEVE
▷ **34** Fold up bottom edge by ¼ in (6 mm). Stitch. Fold with right sides together. Stitch ¼ in (6 mm) from edge. Turn to right side.

◁ **35** Push arm into sleeve. Gather sleeve top close to edge. Slip a pinch of filling into the top of the sleeve around the outside of arm. Pull up gathers tight, tucking edges inside. Stitch through gathers into arm top. Set aside.

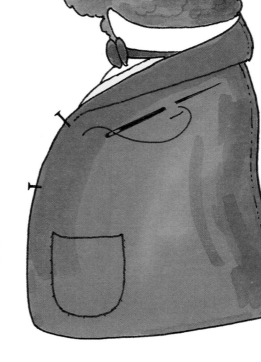

▷ **36** Fold collar ⅝ in (16 mm) over to right side. Iron through a cloth. Wrap coat around bear's back, with collar high at the back. Pin to body at the front. Assess positions for the sleeve tops. At this point, take a couple of stitches through the coat and into the body.

◁ **37** Position sleeve on the coat side. Pin. Take stitches between coat and inner side of sleeve top, where they meet comfortably.

▷ **38** At a point ½ in (13 mm) inside the coat front and level with the collar bottom take a couple of stitches between the inside of the coat and the waistcoat. Pull tight, leaving thread attached. Take the thread through the finger tips, then back through the inside of the coat and out to the right side. Pull up thread and fingers will curl around coat edge. Fasten off thread under the hands.

Bertha BEAR

Before starting work read General Instructions on pages 8, 9 and 10.

Materials

Head and ears Brown fur; see General Instruction 2, page 8.

Eyes Black beads $5/32$ in (4 mm) in diameter.

Nose Black felt.

Shoes Dark brown felt. Stiff card.

Hands Brown felt to match fur.

Body White felt.

Bloomers White cotton.

Dress Printed cotton (small pattern with cream background). Broderie anglaise (tinted cream by dipping in coffee).

Apron and cuffs Cream cotton. Guipure lace $3/8$ in (10 mm) wide (tinted cream by dipping in coffee).

Patchwork Tiny squares of different bright coloured cottons.

Needle Matchstick. Grey felt pen.

Scissors Thick florist's wire (from a florist's shop).

Spectacles 15 amp fuse wire. Clear plastic (the type found in some packaging).

Other materials Polyester fibre toy filling. Strong thread. All-purpose clear adhesive. Threads to match felt.

Patterns

Trace and cut out, keeping to the inside of the line.

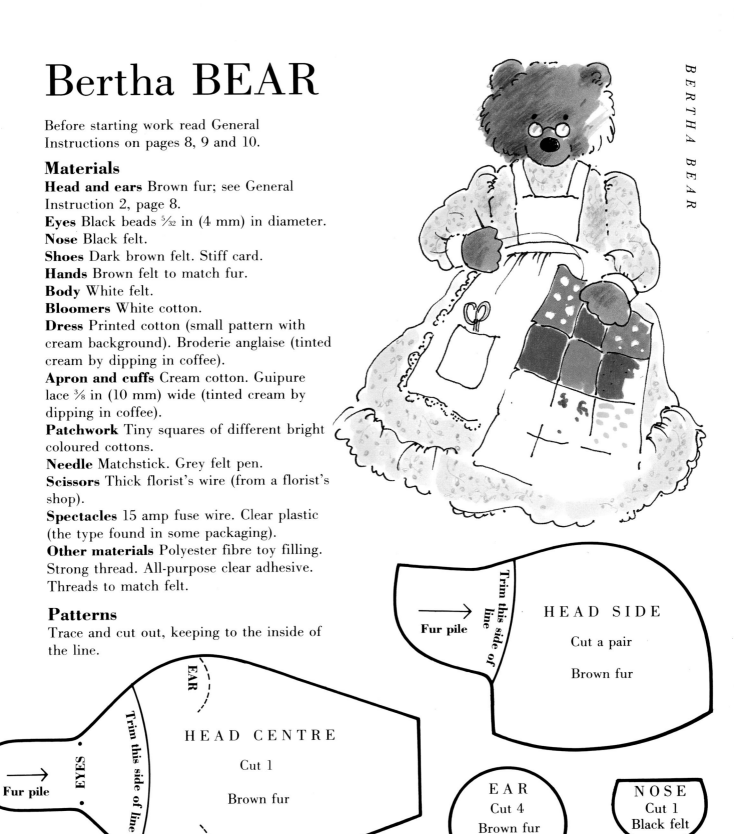

HEAD SIDE

Cut a pair

Brown fur

Trim this side of line

Fur pile

HEAD CENTRE

Cut 1

Brown fur

EAR

EAR

EYES

Fur pile

Trim this side of line

EAR
Cut 4
Brown fur

NOSE
Cut 1
Black felt

51

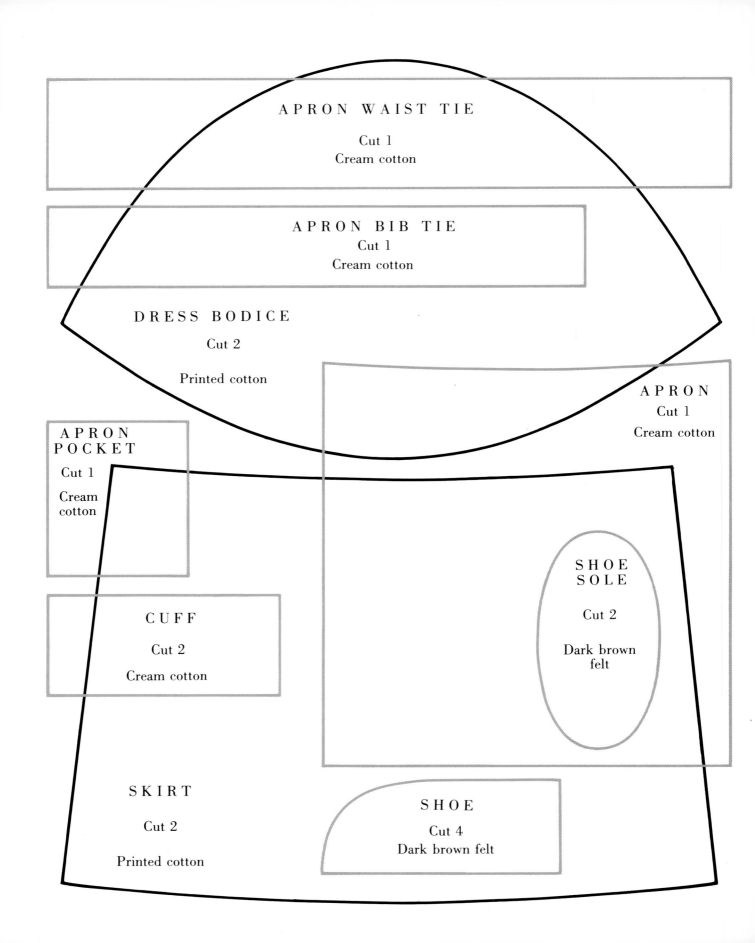

APRON WAIST TIE

Cut 1
Cream cotton

APRON BIB TIE
Cut 1
Cream cotton

DRESS BODICE

Cut 2

Printed cotton

APRON
Cut 1
Cream cotton

APRON
POCKET

Cut 1
Cream
cotton

SHOE
SOLE

Cut 2

Dark brown
felt

CUFF

Cut 2

Cream cotton

SKIRT

Cut 2

Printed cotton

SHOE

Cut 4
Dark brown felt

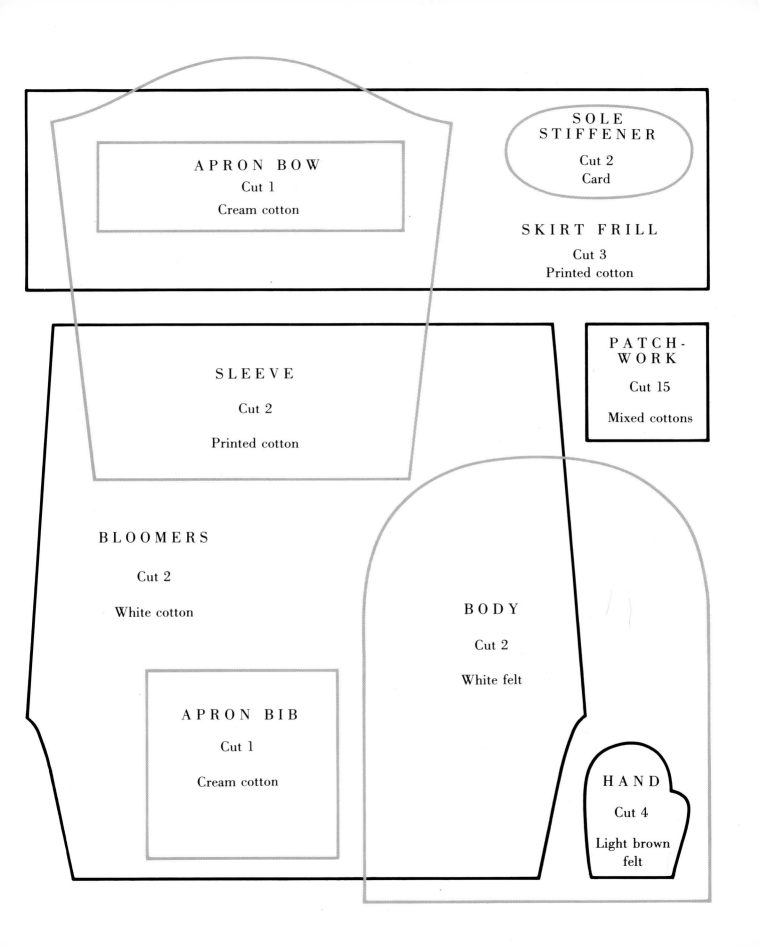

APRON BOW

Cut 1

Cream cotton

SOLE STIFFENER

Cut 2

Card

SKIRT FRILL

Cut 3

Printed cotton

SLEEVE

Cut 2

Printed cotton

PATCH-WORK

Cut 15

Mixed cottons

BLOOMERS

Cut 2

White cotton

BODY

Cut 2

White felt

APRON BIB

Cut 1

Cream cotton

HAND

Cut 4

Light brown felt

Bertha BEAR

Instructions

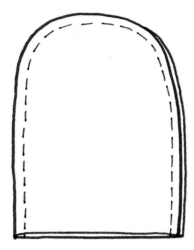

DRESS BODICE

▷ **4** Match pieces. Stitch ¼ in (6 mm) from edge. Trim edge. Turn to right side.

△ **5** Gather around bottom on the edge. Pull bodice over body, with side seams of both matching. Pull up gathers to fit, although the whole bodice will be slightly loose. Stitch through the gathers into the body. Set aside.

SHOES

6 See instructions for Freddie Fox, steps 10–12, page 18. Set aside.

BLOOMERS

▷ **7** Match pieces. Stitch ¼ in (6 mm) from edge.

HEAD, NOSE AND EARS

1 See instructions for Brewster Bear, steps 1–9, pages 43–4, but note that Bertha Bear is slimmer around the base of the head and cheeks.

BODY

◁ **2** Match pieces. Stitch ¼ in (6 mm) from edge. Trim edges close to stitching. Turn to right side.

▷ **3** Fill firmly up to the opening. Take care not to stretch the felt upwards while filling. Gather around opening on the edge. Pull up tight to close. Set aside.

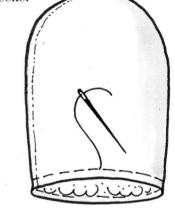

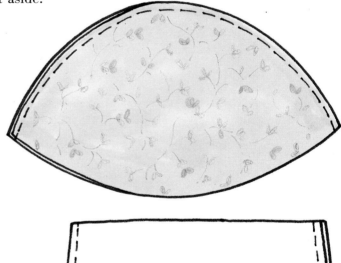

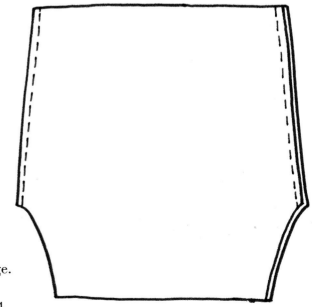

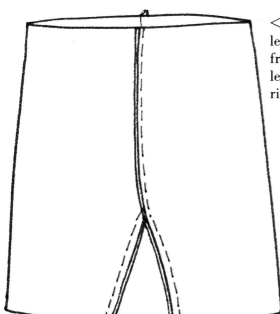

◁ **8** Fold to match inside legs. Stitch ¼ in (6 mm) from edge. Trim inside leg seam edges. Turn to right side.

▷ **9** Gather around leg bottom ¼ in (6 mm) from edge. Pull up tight, tucking edges inside. For Bertha to be sitting down, fill only the bottom 1¼ in (32 mm) of bloomer leg, by wrapping a thread loosely round a pinch of filling. Push this into the leg bottom. Take a stitch up through the gathers, catching filling. Leave remainder of the bloomers empty. Match gathers on shoe to bloomers. Beginning with loose stitches in the centre of both, pull together. Stitch between where they touch. Gather around top of bloomers ¼ in (6 mm) from edge. Fold edge inside on the gather line. Position the body inside, with 2½ in (63 mm) showing above the top of the bloomers. Pull up gathers to fit. Stitch through top of bloomers into body.

▷ **10** For Bertha to be looking downwards, sit head on the front of the body, with the head back just overhanging the centre seam. Beginning with large, loose stitches in the centre of both, pull head to body comfortably. Stitch between where they touch.

SKIRT

▷ **11** Match pieces. Stitch ¼ in (6 mm) from edge. Turn to right side.

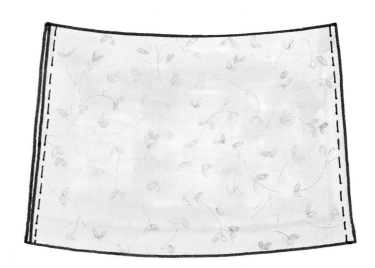

SKIRT FRILL

◁ **12** Match short ends of all three pieces to make a long strip. Stitch ¼ in (6 mm) from edge. Open seams flat. Iron. Fold up bottom edge ¼ in (6 mm) to wrong side. Iron. Match broderie anglaise to wrong side, with edge just showing on the right side. Stitch through lace and hem. Match short ends of frill with right sides together. Stitch. Iron. Gather around frill top ⅛ in (3 mm) from edge. Leave thread attached.

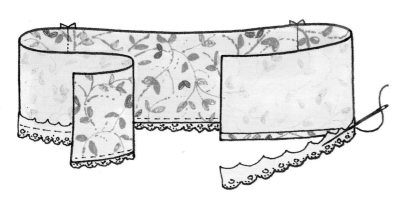

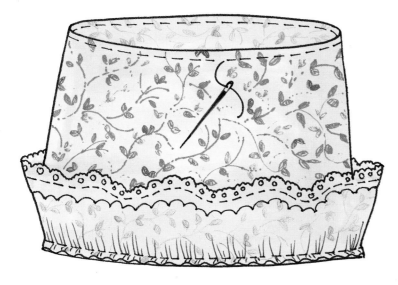

◁ **13** Match frill to skirt bottom with right sides together. Pull up gathers evenly to fit. Pin. Stitch ¼ in (6 mm) from edge. Gather around skirt top ¼ in (6 mm) from edge. Set aside.

HANDS

14 See instructions for Freddie Fox, steps 38 and 39, page 24.

△ SLEEVES

15 Take one piece. Fold up bottom edge by ¼ in (6 mm). Iron. Fold with right sides together. Stitch ¼ in (6 mm) from edge. Turn to right side.

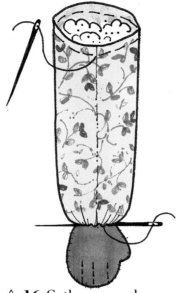

△ 16 Gather around bottom on edge of fold. Pop hand inside with 1 in (25 mm) showing. Pull up gathers to fit around hand. Stitch through gathers into hand. Fill sleeve enough to hold shape. Gather around top ¼ in (6 mm) from edge. Pull up, tucking edges inside.

CUFF

△ 17 Take one piece. Fold long edges to meet in the centre. Iron.

△ 18 Wrap cuff around wrists. Pin. Stitch.

△ 19 Wrap other end over, folding edge inside to fit. Stitch.

◁ 20 Dress body in skirt. Fold top inside on gathers. Pull up gathers to fit tight, pressing well down over bloomers. Stitch through skirt top into body. Position sleeve on the body over the side seam of bodice and ½ in (13 mm) down from head. The right arm will need to be at right angles to the body, and the left arm straight down. Pin. Take stitches between body and inner side of the sleeve top where they touch comfortably. Bend arms at the elbow into a natural position for sewing. Pin. Stitch.

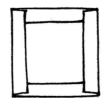

APRON POCKET

△ **21** Fold over all edges by ¼ in (6 mm). Iron.

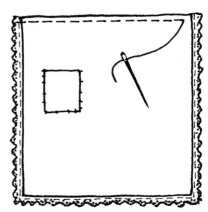

APRON

△ **22** Fold over three edges of apron by ¼ in (6 mm). Iron. Match guipure lace to the right side, allowing it to overhang the edge. Stitch. Position pocket. Stitch. Gather across apron top, ⅛ in (3 mm) from edge. Pull up until it measures 3 in (75 mm).

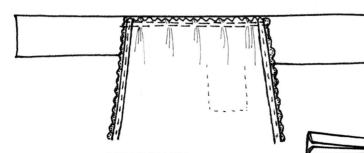

APRON TIE

△ **23** Match wrong side of gathered apron top centrally on apron tie. Stitch ¼ in (6 mm) from edge.

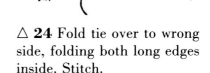

△ **24** Fold tie over to wrong side, folding both long edges inside. Stitch.

BIB TIE

25 Fold over long edges to meet in centre, as cuff. Fold in half again through the length. Finished width ¼ in (6 mm). Iron. Set aside.

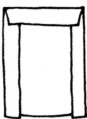

BIB

▷ **26** Fold over three edges by ¼ in (6 mm). Iron.

◁ **27** Lay bib tie around neck. Pin. Position bib over ends. Pin. Stitch top corners and across bottom of bib. Wrap apron around body, pressing well down to skirt top. Stitch through ties at the back.

BOW

△ **28** Fold as bib tie. Iron. Fold overlapping ends in the centre. Stitch. Wrap thread around centre. Pull tight. Glue bow over apron ties at centre back.

SPECTACLES

◁ **29** Cut 2⅝ in (66 mm) length of fuse wire. Wrap one end around a pencil or pen with a ⅜ in (10 mm) diameter. (Check this by wrapping the wire around the object and measuring across the circle.) Pull and pinch the wire tight around the pencil.

◁ **30** Wrap the other end around the pencil in the opposite direction.

△ **31** The finished shape of the spectacles.

△ **32** Grip both circles between finger and thumb. Tilt downwards to move the bridge into the centre and close the circles.

△ **33** Cut two circles of clear plastic slightly bigger than the wire. (This is quite difficult and may need a few tries.) Smear a couple of dots of glue onto the wire. Drop plastic circles on top. Press. Sit specs above the nose. Stitch over the bridge into the fur.

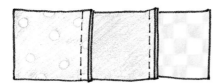

PATCHWORK

△ **34** Lay out the 15 pieces in five rows of three squares. From the first row match pieces one by one. Stitch ¼ in (6 mm) from edge. Open pieces and seams out flat. Iron. Repeat with other four rows.

△ **35** Match two rows. Stitch ¼ in (6 mm) from edge. Open out. Iron. Repeat with other rows.

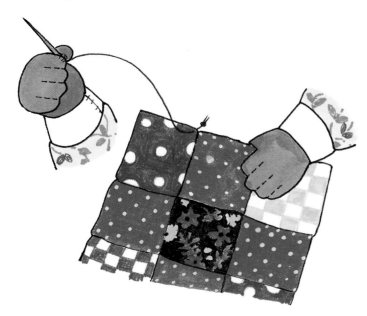

NEEDLE AND THREAD

◁ **36** To make the needle, shave a matchstitck with a craft knife until pointed and smooth and cut it to ¾ in (19 mm) long. Colour with grey felt pen. Put a spot of glue near the blunt end and wrap with a piece of strong thread. Stitch other end of thread through patchwork. Cut thread down to 3½ in (89 mm). Position needle in raised hand. Bend thumb to finger. Stitch between. Position patchwork in the other hand. Stitch.

▽ **39** Twist both top curves in opposite direction, bringing the two straight wires together in the centre. Hold scissors in pocket with a stitch through the back of the apron.

SCISSORS

▽ **37** Cut a 4 in (100 mm) piece of thick florist's wire. Bend in half.

▽ **38** Bend top over by ½ in (13 mm) keeping all lines parallel.

Kenny
·KOALA·

Kenny KOALA

Before starting the work read General Instructions on pages 8, 9 and 10.

Materials

Head, ears, arms and legs Grey speckled fur; see General Instruction 2, page 8.

Chest and ear tufts White fur.

Eyes Black beads $\frac{5}{32}$ in (4 mm) in diameter.

Nose Black felt.

Body, legs, shoes and laces White felt. Stiff card. Thick white thread.

Shirt Bright coloured dress fabric. Tiny buttons (from a shop selling doll-making materials).

Shorts Cream cotton (curtain lining).

Hat, band and corks Light brown felt. Brown suede (old suede skirt). Balsa wood dowel $\frac{1}{4}$ in (6 mm) diameter (bought from model shop). Strong black thread.

Other materials Polyester fibre toy filling. All-purpose clear adhesive.

Patterns

Trace and cut out, keeping to the inside of the line.

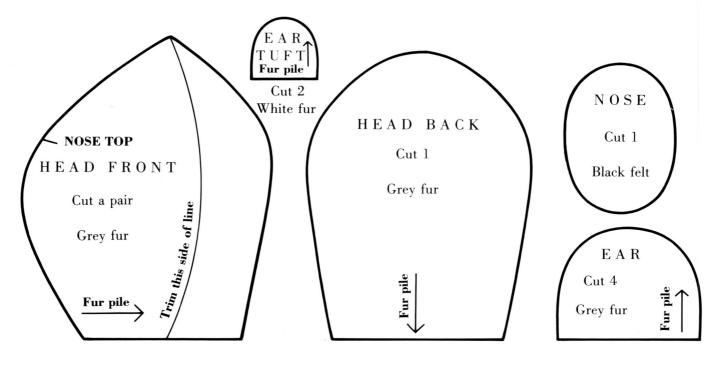

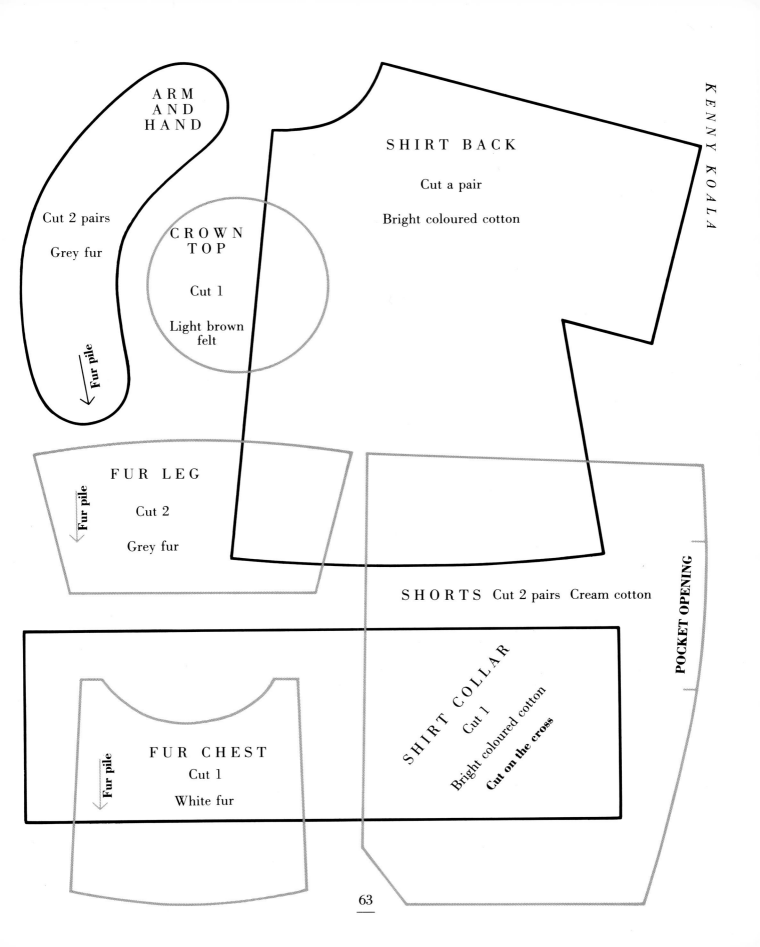

ARM
AND
HAND

Cut 2 pairs

Grey fur

Fur pile

CROWN
TOP

Cut 1

Light brown
felt

SHIRT BACK

Cut a pair

Bright coloured cotton

KENNY KOALA

FUR LEG

Cut 2

Grey fur

Fur pile

SHORTS   Cut 2 pairs   Cream cotton

POCKET OPENING

FUR CHEST

Cut 1

White fur

Fur pile

SHIRT COLLAR

Cut 1

Bright coloured cotton

Cut on the cross

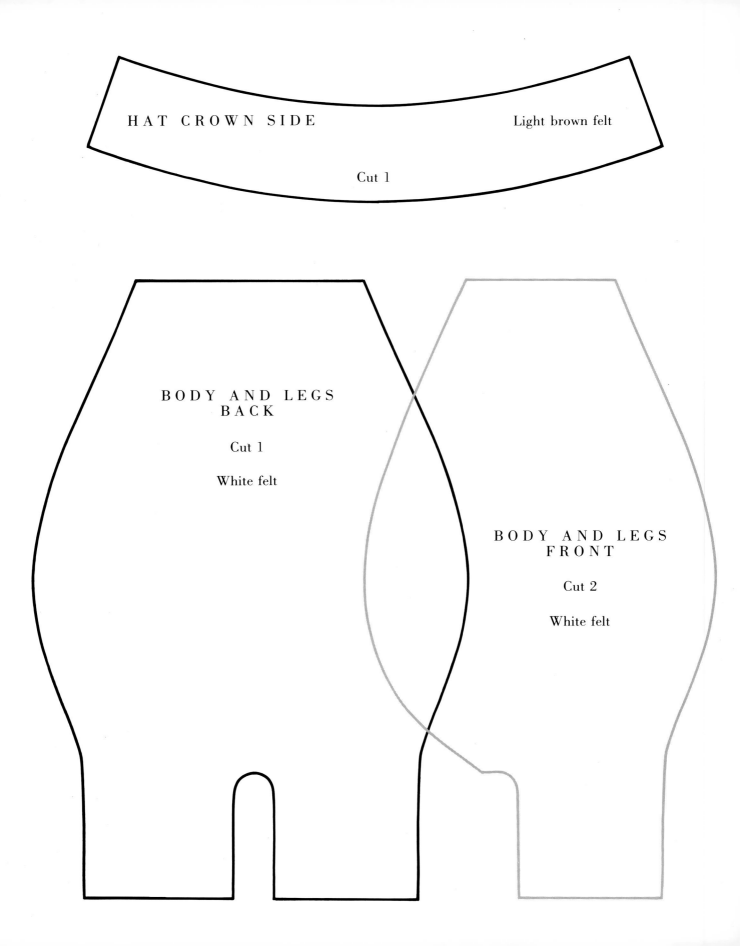

HAT CROWN SIDE

Light brown felt

Cut 1

BODY AND LEGS
BACK

Cut 1

White felt

BODY AND LEGS
FRONT

Cut 2

White felt

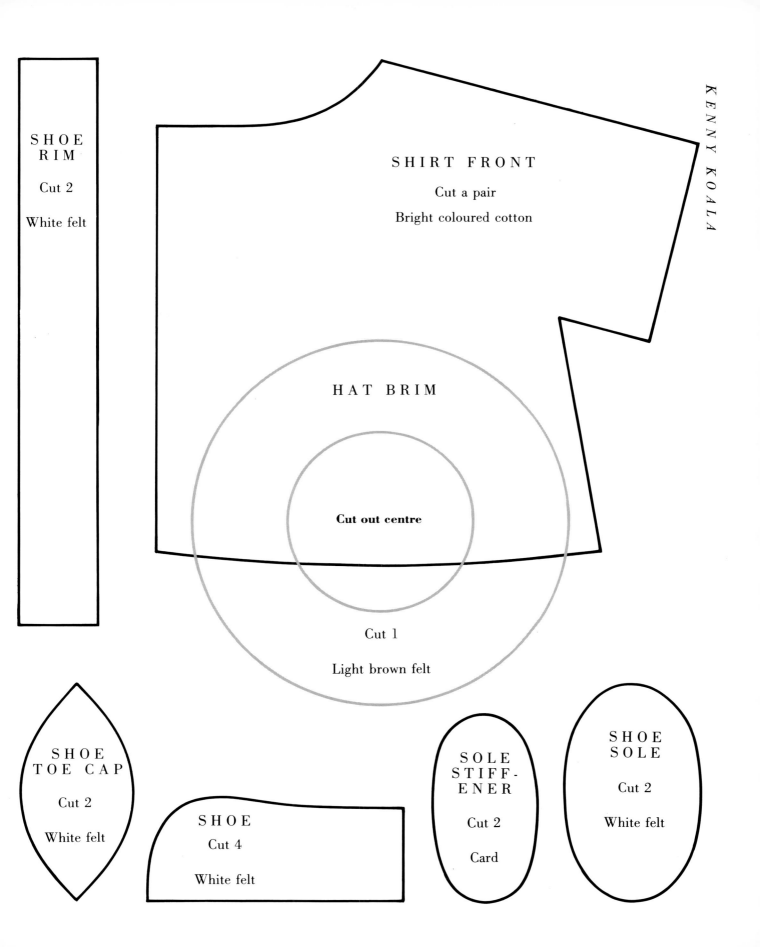

SHOE
RIM

Cut 2

White felt

SHIRT FRONT

Cut a pair

Bright coloured cotton

KENNY KOALA

HAT BRIM

Cut out centre

Cut 1

Light brown felt

SHOE
TOE CAP

Cut 2

White felt

SHOE

Cut 4

White felt

SOLE
STIFF-
ENER

Cut 2

Card

SHOE
SOLE

Cut 2

White felt

Kenny KOALA

Instructions

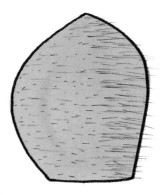

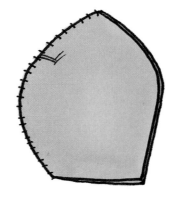

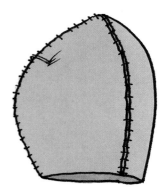

HEAD

△ **1** Trim fur pile on both head front pieces as shown on pattern.

△ **2** Match head front pieces. Oversew edge. Open out flat. Take a large, loose stitch between nose marks, to show on the right side.

△ **3** Match head back into head fronts. Ease together. Pin. Beginning at the centre top and working downwards, oversew edges. Turn to right side.

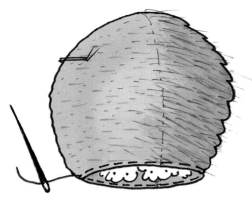

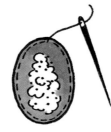

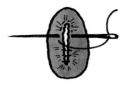

NOSE

△ **5** Gather around on the edge. Fill centre, putting more filling at the bottom than top.

△ **4** Fill head until well rounded, especially the face centre. Gather on the edge. Pull up tight to close. Set aside.

△ **6** Pull gathers until edges just touch. Stitch from side to side across opening. Flatten nose top by squeezing back to front. Set aside.

EARS

▷ **7** Take two ear pieces. Trim fur pile very short. Match one short to one long piece. Pin. Tuck fur pile inside with the point of the needle. Oversew edge. Turn to right side.

△ **8** Oversew across bottom edge, pulling stitches tight to curve the edge slightly.

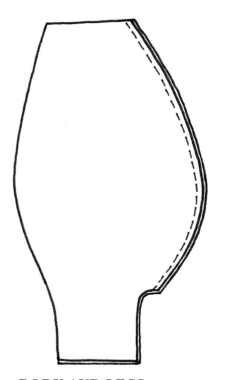

△ **9** Position ears so they stand up on the head seam, 2 in (50 mm) apart and with the short fur facing forwards. Pin. Stitch through bottom of ears into head. Smear a small dot of glue on the back of the white ear tuft. Press tuft well into the ear front. Position nose on face, with the top touching the marker stitch. Stitch side to side through the back of the nose into the face. Position and stitch eyes level with the nose top and with the centres 1 in (25 mm) apart.

BODY AND LEGS
△ **10** Match front pieces. Stitch ¼ in (6 mm) from the edge. Open out flat.

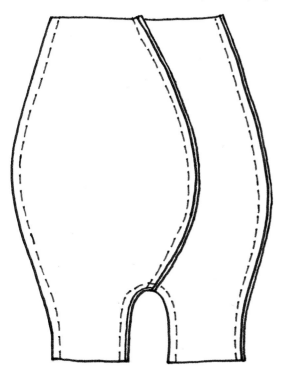

◁ **11** Match fronts to back piece. Stitch. Trim edges close to stitching. Turn to right side.

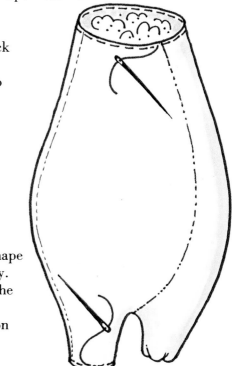

▷ **12** Fill firmly up to openings, rounding the shape well, especially the tummy. Take care not to stretch the felt upwards while filling. Gather around openings on the edge. Pull up tight to close.

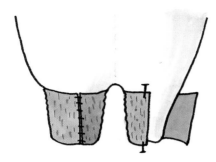

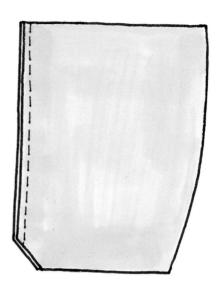

FUR LEGS

△ **13** Trim fur pile very short all over both leg pieces. Wrap one piece tightly around leg, the bottom edge level with bottom of leg. Butt edges at the back. Trim to fit. Pin. Stitch across edges and into leg.

SHORTS

△ **14** Match two pieces. Stitch ¼ in (6 mm) from edge. Open out. Iron. Repeat with other two pieces.

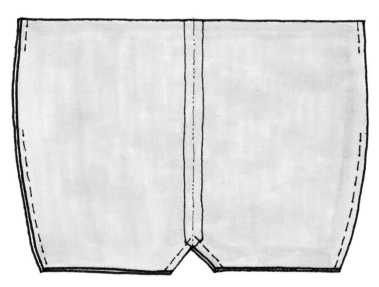

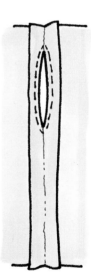

△ **15** Match pieces. Stitch between legs and side seams, leaving pocket openings as marked on pattern. Trim edges between legs.

△ **16** Open side seams flat. Iron. Stitch around pockets. Turn to right side.

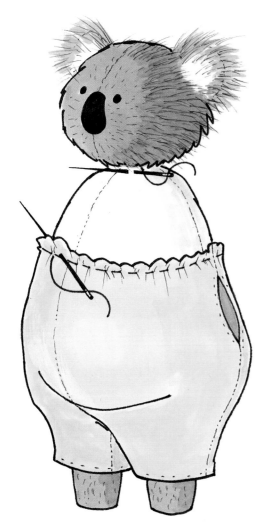

◁ **17** Fold bottom edge of shorts ¼ in (6 mm) to wrong side. Stitch invisibly. Gather around top. Dress body in shorts, pulling them well up. Slip a small amount of filling into the back of shorts to round the bottom. Pull up gathers to fit. Stitch around top into body. Sit head on body. Beginning with large, loose stitches in the centre of body, pull head to body comfortably. Stitch between where they touch.

SHOES
△ **18** Match two pieces. Oversew edge using tiny, close stitches, pulled tight. Leave 1 in (25 mm) of top open and bottom open.

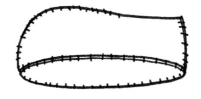

△ **19** Ease sole into shoe. Pin. Oversew edge. Turn to right side.

△ **20** Position card sole in shoe. Fill firmly to the top. Gather around on the edge. Pull up tight.

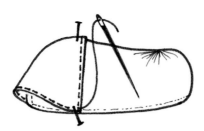
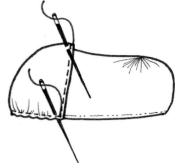

TOE CAP

△ **21** Take one piece. For decoration, stitch close to one edge with white thread.

△ **22** Gather very close to other edge. Pull toe cap tightly over the shoe with gathered edge to the bottom. Pin corners and top. Pull up gathers to fit tight around sole edge.

△ **23** Stitch through gathers into edge of sole. Stitch through the top into the shoe.

SHOE RIM

△ **24** Take one shoe rim piece and fold in half through the length. Check the rim fits tightly around shoe with the ends butted together. Trim to fit. For decoration, stitch ⅛ in (3 mm) from the fold with white thread. Trim edge, leaving rim ¼ in (6 mm) deep.

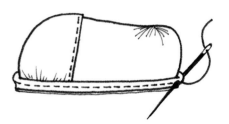

△ **25** Position tightly around shoe. Pin. Stitch into shoe at back and front.

◁ **26** Press bottom of leg over gathers on shoe top, with toes pointing slightly outwards. Pin. Stitch around where they touch, pulling together.

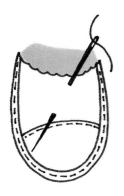 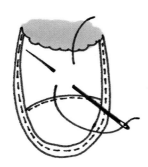  

△ **27** With a thick white thread, stitch side to side to form laces. Tie ends into a bow.

HAT

△ **28** Fold hat crown side to match short edges. Oversew edge.

△ **29** Match crown top to the sides. Oversew edge. Turn to right side. Squeeze and pinch seams to flatten.

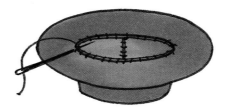

△ **30** Lay brim over crown. Oversew edge. Set aside.

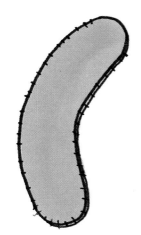

ARMS AND HANDS

◁ **31** Trim fur pile very short on all pieces. Match one pair with right sides together. Oversew edge leaving top open. Turn to right side.

▷ **32** Gather around wrists ¾ in (19 mm) from end. Pull up slightly. Do not fill hand. Fill arm softly up to 1 in (25 mm) from the top. Oversew across top edges.

FUR CHEST

◁ **33** Lay piece on chest, high under chin. Pin. Stitch top corners and across bottom edge. Position arm tops over side seams of body ½ in (13 mm) from the head. Pin. Stitch through top into body. Sit hat on top of head. Lift brim up. Pin. Stitch through brim/crown stitches into head. Take care not to pull stitches tight or you will distort the brim. Repeat at the back.

HATBAND

◁ **34** Cut three lengths of suede ⅛ x 7¼ in (3 x 184 mm). Bind ends with thread. Pin end to the arm of a chair. Plait evenly. Bind ends with thread. Lay around the crown. Glue ends at the back.

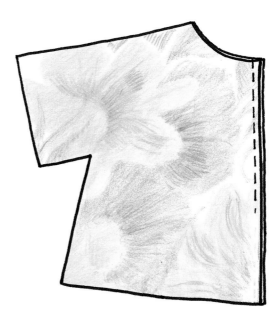

CORKS

△ **35** From a balsa wood dowel ¼ in (6 mm) in diameter, cut four ½ in (13 mm) lengths with a craft knife. Push a pin in the dowel to hold while you work. Colour wood with a light brown felt pen. Mark a few dots with a darker pen. Wrap black thread around cork, tie knot. Stitch other end to hat brim so that corks hang level with eyes.

SHIRT

△ **36** Match back pieces. Stitch ¼ in (6 mm) from edge, stopping 1¼ in (32 mm) from the bottom. Open out flat including the seam. Iron.

◁ **37** Match shirt fronts to back piece. Stitch. Clip into seam edges under the arms.

COLLAR
△ **38** Fold in half through length. Stitch ¼ in (6 mm) from the edge. Trim edges. Turn to right side. Iron.

△ **39** Match centre of collar to the right side of the back centre seam of shirt. Stitch ¼ in (6 mm) from edge.

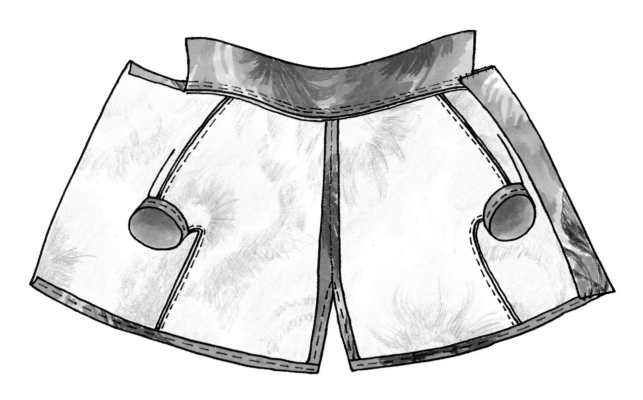

△ **40** Stand collar up. To hold in that position, stitch through all layers of collar and shirt neck below the previous row of stitches.

For simplicity, the next instructions are shown on the wrong side of the shirt. The stitching is, however, best done from the right side so that you are sure that the stitches do not show. Fold up bottom of sleeve by ¼ in (6 mm). Stitch. Stitch edges of centre back opening to form a vent. Fold up bottom edge of shirt by ¼ in (6 mm). Stitch. Fold down remaining neck edge to wrong side. Fold front edges ¾ in (19 mm) to wrong side. Oversew across top and bottom. Iron by touching the seams with just the point of the iron. Dress body in shirt. Overlap fronts to fit. Stitch. Position buttons. Stitch. Pop hands into pocket.

Reggie and Rosie
·RABBIT·

Reggie RABBIT

Before starting work read General Instructions on pages 8, 9 and 10.

Materials

Head and ears Brown fur; see General Instruction 2, page 8. White embroidery thread.
Cheeks and tail White fur.
Eyes Black beads ⁵⁄₃₂ in (4 mm) in diameter.
Nose, hands and arms Brown felt to match fur.
Body and legs White felt.
Shoes and hatband Dark brown felt. Stiff card.
Waistcoat Green felt. Thread to match.
Ladybird Red felt. Black embroidery thread.
Trousers Heavy cotton drill (old overalls). String.
Shirt Check cotton (man's shirt).
Neckerchief Red spotted cotton.
Hat Calico.
Broom Wooden dowel ³⁄₁₆ in (5 mm) in diameter (from woodwork shop). Fine twigs. String.
Other materials Polyester fibre toy filling. Strong thread. All-purpose clear adhesive. Threads to match felt.

Patterns

Trace and cut out, keeping to the inside of the line.

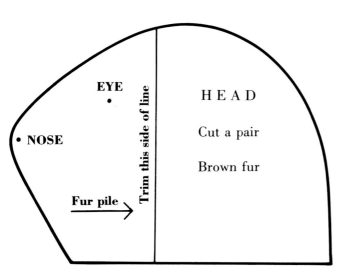

HEAD

Cut a pair

Brown fur

EYE

• NOSE

Trim this side of line

Fur pile →

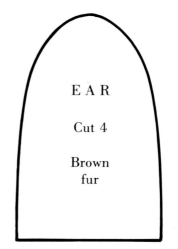

EAR

Cut 4

Brown fur

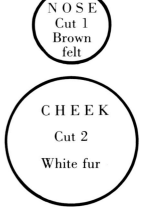

NOSE
Cut 1
Brown felt

CHEEK
Cut 2
White fur

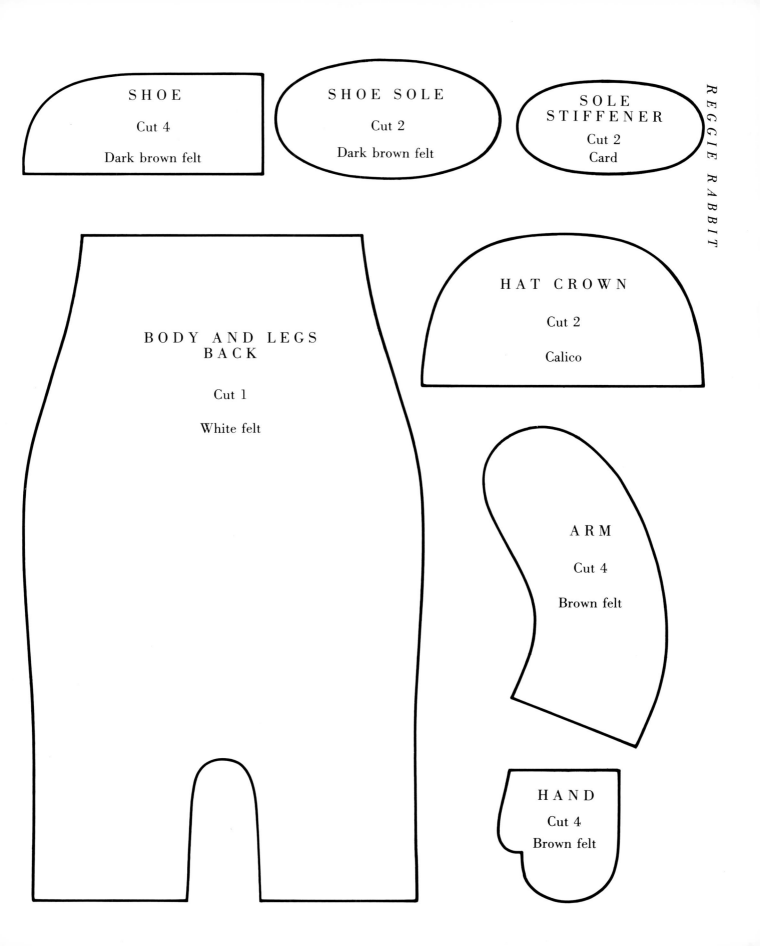

SHOE

Cut 4

Dark brown felt

SHOE SOLE

Cut 2

Dark brown felt

SOLE
STIFFENER

Cut 2

Card

BODY AND LEGS
BACK

Cut 1

White felt

HAT CROWN

Cut 2

Calico

ARM

Cut 4

Brown felt

HAND

Cut 4

Brown felt

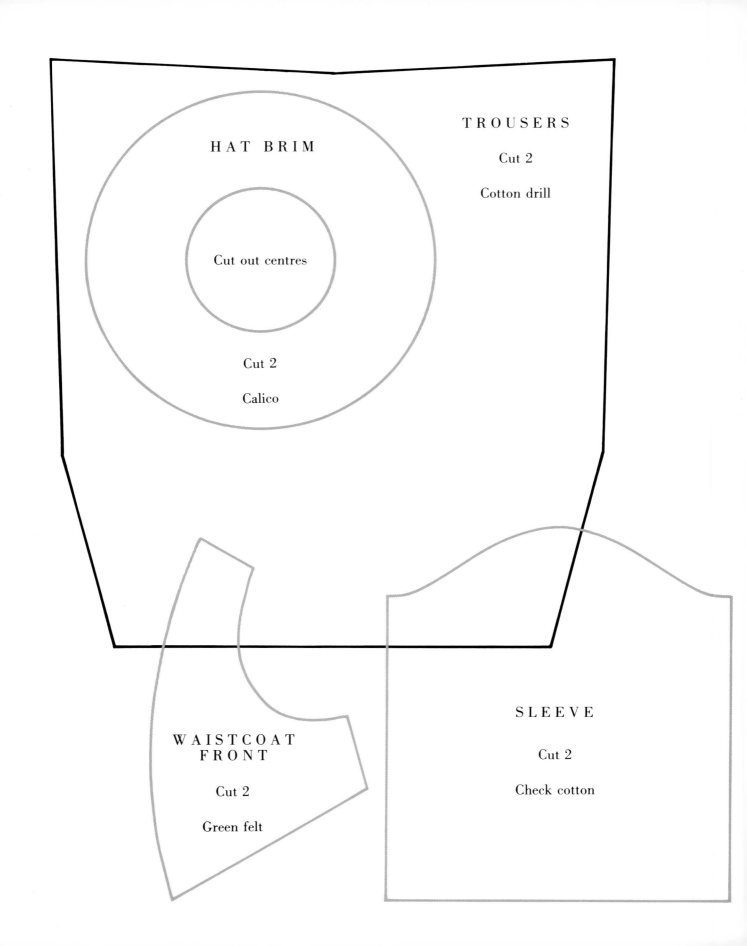

HAT BRIM

Cut out centres

Cut 2

Calico

TROUSERS

Cut 2

Cotton drill

WAISTCOAT
FRONT

Cut 2

Green felt

SLEEVE

Cut 2

Check cotton

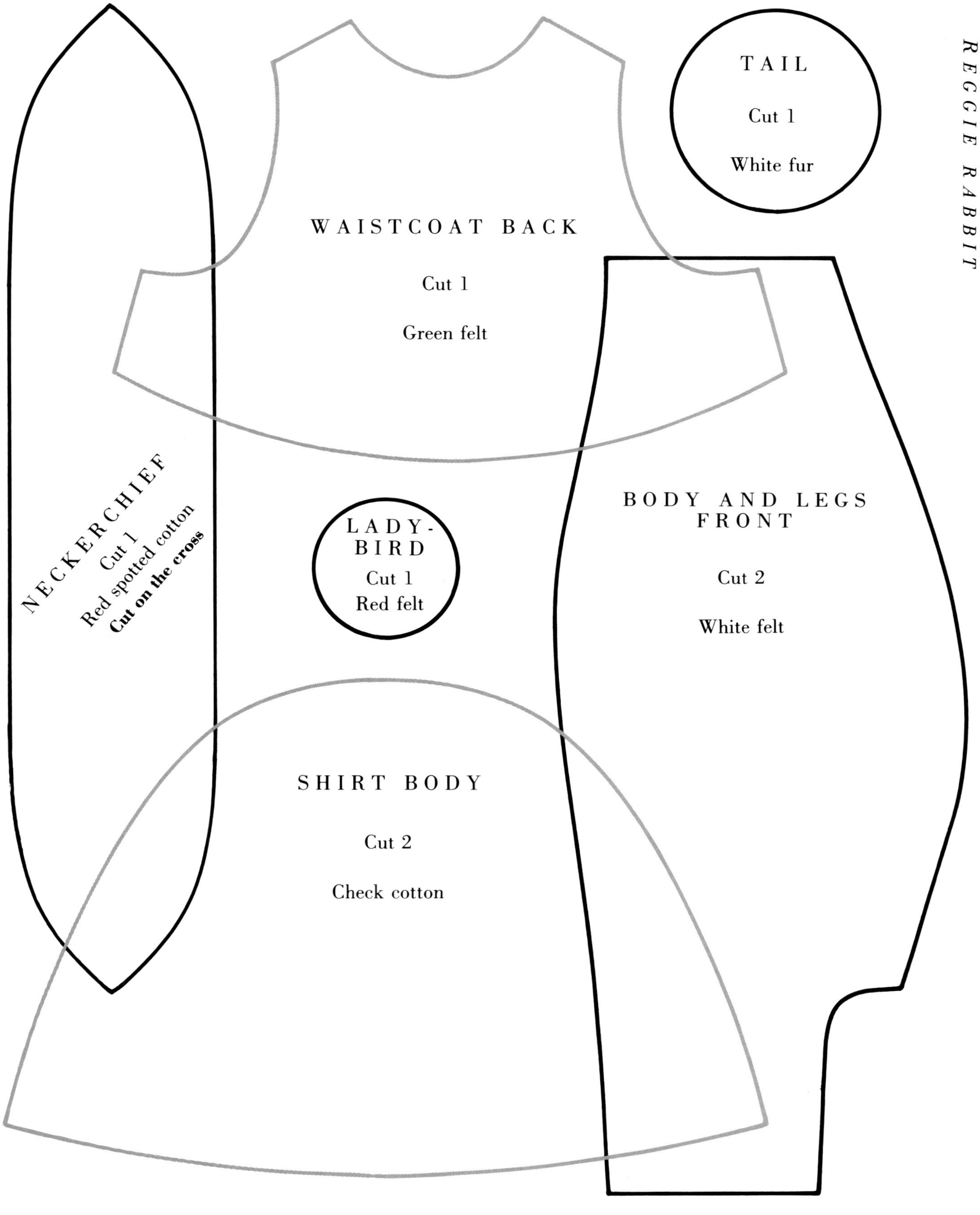

TAIL

Cut 1

White fur

WAISTCOAT BACK

Cut 1

Green felt

BODY AND LEGS
FRONT

Cut 2

White felt

NECKERCHIEF

Cut 1

Red spotted cotton

Cut on the cross

LADY-
BIRD

Cut 1
Red felt

SHIRT BODY

Cut 2

Check cotton

Reggie RABBIT

Instructions

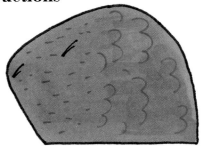

HEAD

△ **1** Trim fur pile on both pieces as shown on pattern. Mark positions of eyes and nose.

△ **2** Match head pieces. Oversew edge. Turn to right side.

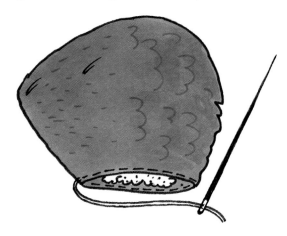

△ **3** Fill head until well rounded and firm. With 36 in (915 mm) length of strong thread used double in a long darning needle, gather head around bottom on the edge. Pull up tight. Fasten off but leave needle and thread attached.

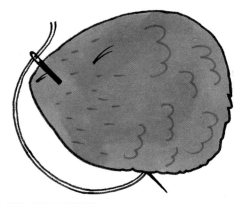

FACE SHAPING

△ **4** The next few stitches will lie on top of the fur but will disappear into the pile when they are pulled tight. To help, pinch the head as you pull in the thread. If the results are not shapely enough, repeat the process. Don't worry if the head looks odd while shaping. Pull each stitch tight as you work. Take the needle down through the face ½ in (13 mm) to the side of the nose mark and then out through the gathers under the head. Pull tight to indent face.

FRONT VIEW

◁ **5** Repeat on the other side of the face.

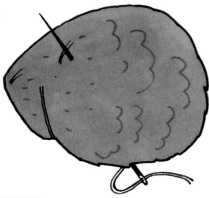

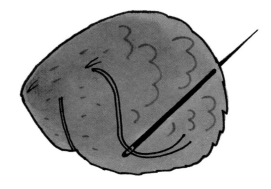

SIDE VIEW

△ **6** Take needle up through gathers and out ¼ in (6 mm) behind eye mark.

△ **7** Take a small stitch through the back of the head.

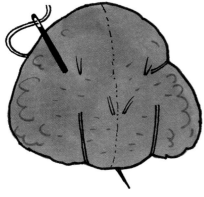

FRONT VIEW

△ **8** Take the needle into the other side of the head ¼ in (6 mm) behind the eye mark, then out through the gathers. Pull tight. Fasten off.

NOSE

△ **9** Gather on edge. Pull up tight to close.

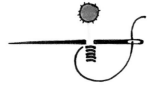

△ **10** Stitch back and forth over the gathers, pulling tight. Squeeze nose flat. Nose should measure ⅜ in (10 mm) across.

△ **11** Position nose on face over mark. Pin. Stitch around nose into face. Build up small teeth ¼ in (6 mm) down from the nose by stitching over and over with white embroidery thread.

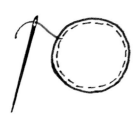
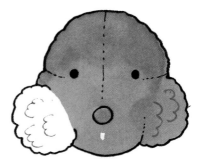

CHEEKS

△ **12** Take one piece. Gather on edge. Pull up tight. Squash flat.

△ **13** Cheeks can be stitched to face but glue is better. Put a few spots of glue on the centre of back and press to the face. Stitch bead eyes over marks.

BODY AND LEGS

14 See instructions for Kenny Koala, steps 10–12, page 67, but note that Reggie Rabbit is taller and his tummy is smaller. Set aside.

SHOES

15 See instructions for Freddie Fox, steps 10–12, page 18.

SHIRT BODY

16 See instructions for Freda Fox's blouse bodice, steps 2 and 3, page 32.

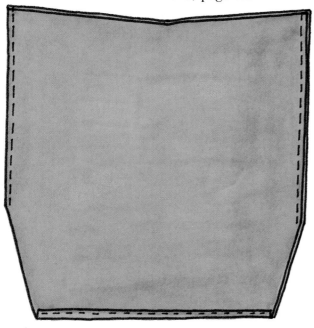
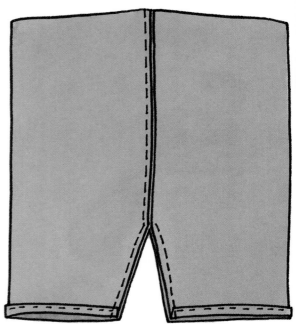

TROUSERS

△ **17** Take one piece. Fold up bottom edge by ¼ in (6 mm). Stitch. Repeat with other piece. Match pieces. Stitch ¼ in (6 mm) from edge.

△ **18** Fold to match inside legs. Stitch ¼ in (6 mm) from edge. Trim inside legs close to stitching. Turn to right side.

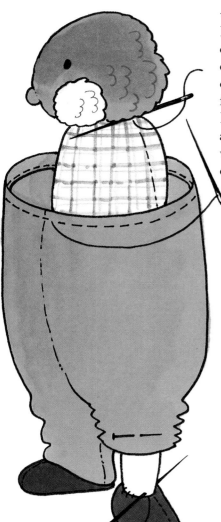

◁ **19** Dress body in trousers. Push trouser legs up out of the way. Pin. Press leg bottom over gathers on shoe top, with toes pointing slightly outwards. Pin. Stitch around twice, pulling together. Slip small pinches of filling into the trousers at the back to shape the bottom. Fold top over ¼ in (6 mm) to wrong side. Gather around just under ¼ in (6 mm) from fold, stitching through both layers of fabric. Pull trousers well up. Pull up gathers to fit body. Stitch through gathers into body. Tie string around over the gathers. Knot at the front. Sit head on body. Beginning with large, loose stitches in the centre of both, pull head to body comfortably. Stitch between where they touch.

TAIL
20 Make the tail in the same way as the cheeks, step 12, page 82. Stitch to centre seam of trouser back.

HANDS AND ARMS
21 See instructions for Freddie Fox, steps 38–42, page 24, but note that Reggie Rabbit's arms are stronger than Freddie Fox's. Fill slightly firmer and stitch hands to arms neatly because the join will show.

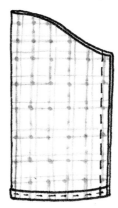

SLEEVES
△ **22** Fold up bottom edge by ¼ in (6 mm). Iron. Stitch. Fold to match edges. Stitch ¼ in (6 mm) from the edge. Turn to right side.

△ **23** Push arm into sleeve. Pin. Gather around sleeve top on the edge. Pull up tight, tucking edges inside.

◁ **24** Stitch through gathers into top of arm. Wrinkle up sleeve and stitch bottom edge to the inside of arm. Set aside.

HAT BRIM
▷ **25** Match pieces. Stitch ¼ in (6 mm) from edge. Trim edge.

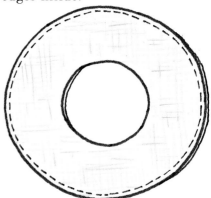

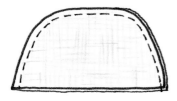

CROWN

◁ **26** Match pieces. Stitch ¼ in (6 mm) from edge. Trim edge. Turn to right side.

◁ **27** Ease crown edges into hole in centre of brim. Oversew edges.

▷ **28** Sit hat well forwards on top of head, with the crown seam running from side to side. Stitch through brim/crown seam into head. A few stitches will hold. Do not pull too tight or you will distort the brim. Dent the crown. For the hatband cut a piece of brown felt 4 x ¼ in (100 x 6 mm). Glue around crown. Position sleeve on side of body ½ in (13 mm) down from head. Pin. Take stitches between body and inner side of the sleeve top, where they touch comfortably.

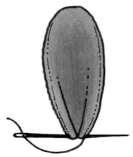

EARS

△ **29** Trim fur pile very short on all pieces. Match two pieces. Oversew edge. Turn to right side. Iron through a cloth.

△ **30** Match bottom corners together. Stitch.

▷ **31** Stretch hat brim flat over head back. Pin. Position ears standing up, facing forwards on the brim behind and pressed close to the crown. Stitch through ear bottoms and through brim, catching the head with a couple of stitches. This is quite difficult without making the brim wavy. To keep ears upright, take a stitch through the crown into the ears where they touch.

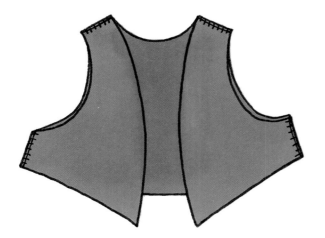

WAISTCOAT

△ **32** Match both front pieces to the back piece. Oversew edges. Turn to right side. Flatten seams.

△ **33** Stitch all around waistcoat, close to the edges with a thread the same colour as the felt. Dress body in waistcoat.

NECKERCHIEF

△ **34** The edges of the neckerchief will be left unhemmed. Handle carefully, so they do not fray. Gather ends 1¼ in (32 mm) from the points. Pull up loosely.

▷ **35** Wrap around neck. Take a stitch through both ends at the gathers to hold together.

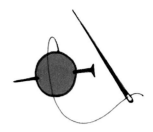

LADYBIRD

△ **36** Use strong thread to gather around edge. Fill centre. Pull up tight.

△ **37** To make the shape smaller and tighter, gather around over the previous gathers, pulling tight again. Keep going until shape measures ⅜ in (10 mm) across. Squash flatter.

△ **38** Push in a pin to hold while you work. Wrap a black thread tightly around the centre.

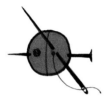

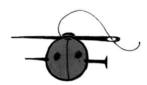

△ **39** Make spots by closely grouping tiny stitches in black embroidery thread.

△ **40** To make head, make three short stitches on top of each other.

△ **41** Take needle around the three stitches to build an even shape that is larger in the centre. Glue or stitch the ladybird to hat brim.

BROOM

◁ **42** Cut a piece of wooden dowel ³⁄₁₆ in (5 mm) in diameter to 5½ in (139 mm) long. Cut a small bundle of fine twigs measuring 6 in (150 mm) long. Sandpaper one end of the dowel to round the edges. Apply glue to the last ¾ in (19 mm) of the other end. Push glued end into the centre of the bunch of twigs, squeeze until dry. Wrap string around very tight. Tie knot. Trim twigs level across the bottom. Wrap hands around handle in a natural sweeping position. Stitch between finger tips and palms around broom handle.

Rosie RABBIT

Before starting work read General Instructions on pages 8, 9 and 10.

Materials

Head and ears Brown fur, see General Instruction 2, page 8. White embroidery thread.

Tail White fur.

Eyes Black beads $5/32$ in (4 mm) in diameter.

Nose Brown felt to match fur.

Body, legs and hands White felt. Fine lace $1/4$ in (6 mm) wide.

Shoes Dark brown felt. Stiff card.

Hat White linen (from old skirt).

Collar Fine white cotton.

Dress Printed cotton.

Bloomers White cotton.

Basket $2\frac{1}{2}$ in (63 mm) high (bought from florist's shop).

Roses Paper handkerchief tissue. Pink felt pen. Thick florist's wire.

Leaves Green tissue, napkin or crepe paper.

Other materials Polyester fibre toy filling. All-purpose clear adhesive. Strong thread. Threads to match felt.

Patterns

Trace and cut, keeping to the inside of the line.

NOSE
Cut 1

Light brown felt

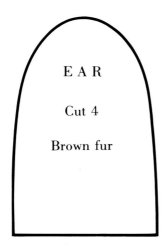

EAR

Cut 4

Brown fur

EYE

• NOSE

Fur pile →

Trim this side of line

HEAD

Cut a pair

Brown fur

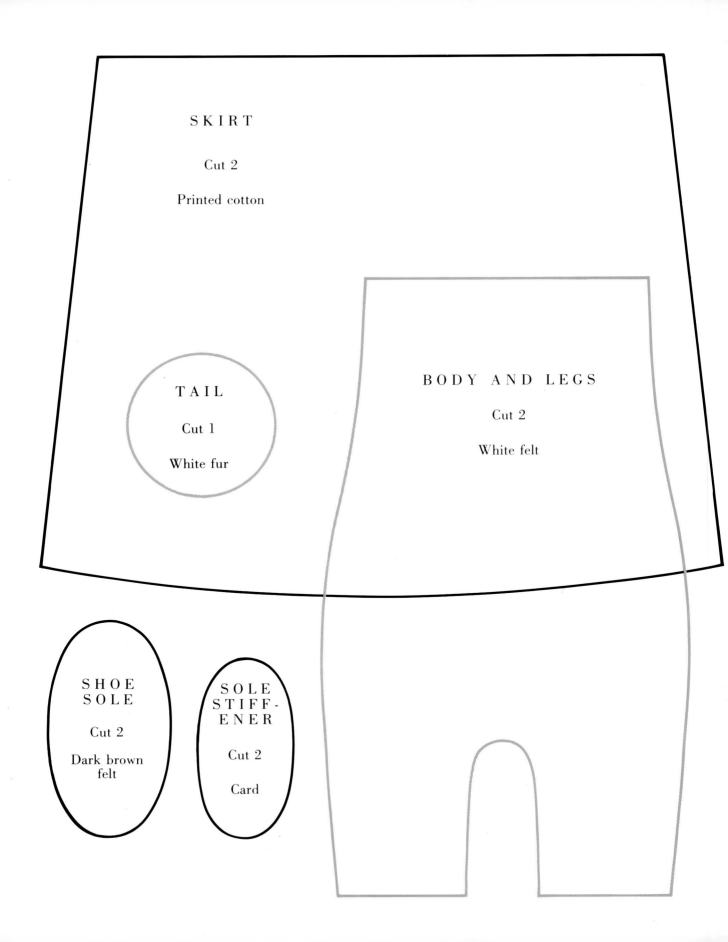

S K I R T

Cut 2

Printed cotton

T A I L

Cut 1

White fur

B O D Y   A N D   L E G S

Cut 2

White felt

S H O E
S O L E

Cut 2

Dark brown
felt

S O L E
S T I F F -
E N E R

Cut 2

Card

HAND

Cut 4

White felt

HAT BRIM

Cut out centre of one piece

Cut 2

White linen

BLOOMERS

Cut 2

White cotton

HAT CROWN

Cut 1

White linen

SLEEVE

Cut 2

Printed cotton

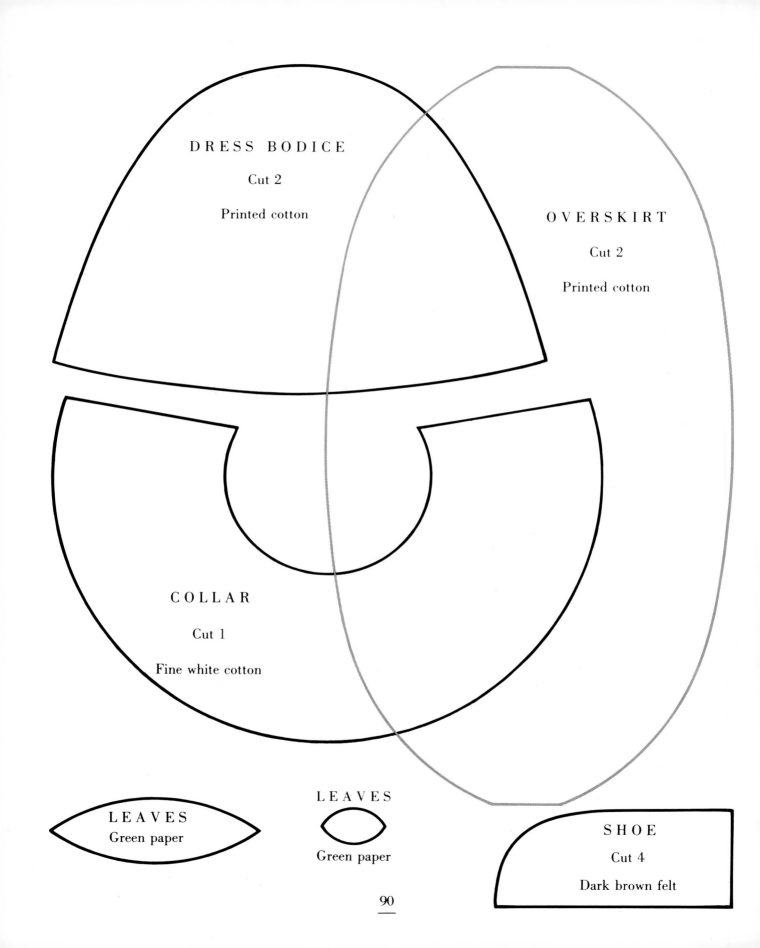

DRESS BODICE

Cut 2

Printed cotton

OVERSKIRT

Cut 2

Printed cotton

COLLAR

Cut 1

Fine white cotton

LEAVES
Green paper

LEAVES

Green paper

SHOE

Cut 4

Dark brown felt

Rosie RABBIT

Instructions

HEAD, FACE SHAPING AND NOSE

1 See instructions for Reggie Rabbit, steps 1–9, pages 80–81. Stitch back and forth across nose gathers pulling tight. Squeeze nose flat. Nose should measure ¼ in (6 mm) across.

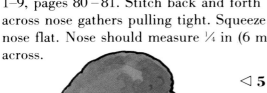

TEETH, NOSE AND EYES

2 See instructions for Reggie Rabbit, step 11, page 81. Stitch bead eyes over marks.

SHOES, BODY AND LEGS

3 See instructions for Freddie Fox, steps 10–14, pages 18–19.

DRESS BODICE AND BLOOMERS

4 See instructions for Bertha Bear, steps 4–8, pages 54–5.

◁ **5** Dress body in bloomers. Push bloomer legs up out of the way. Pin. Press bottom of leg over gathers on shoe top, with toes pointing slightly outwards. Pin. Stitch around twice, pulling together. Slip small pinches of filling into the bloomers at the back. Gather top ¼ in (6 mm) from the edge. Fold inside on the gathers. Pull up to fit. Stitch through top into body. Gather around bottom of bloomer leg ¼ in (6 mm) from edge. Fold inside on gathers. Pull up gathers to fit. Hold to shoe top with a stitch. Sit head on body. Beginning with large, loose stitches in the centre of both, pull head to body comfortably. Stitch between where they touch.

TAIL

▷ **6** Gather on edge. Pull up tight. Squash flat. Stitch tail to centre back of bloomers.

SKIRT

▷ **7** Match pieces. Stitch sides ¼ in (6 mm) from edge. Fold up bottom by ¼ in (6 mm). Stitch. Gather around top, leaving thread attached. Turn to right side. Iron. Dress body in skirt. Fold top edge inside on gathers. Pull up gathers to fit, pressing well down over bloomers top. Stitch through top into body.

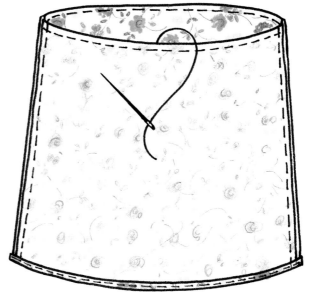

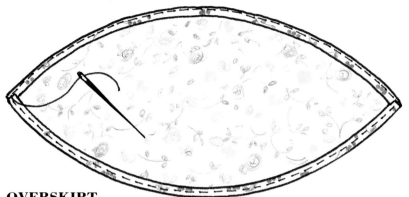

OVERSKIRT

△ **8** Take one piece. Fold edges over by ¼ in (6 mm). Pin. Stitch bottom edge invisibly. Gather across top through both layers of fabric on the edge of the fold. Leave needle and thread attached. Repeat with other piece. Set aside.

HANDS

9 See instructions for Freddie Fox, steps 38 and 39, page 24.

SLEEVES

△ **10** Take one piece. Fold up bottom edge by ¼ in (6 mm). Iron. Fold to match edges. Stitch ¼ in (6 mm) from edge. Turn to right side.

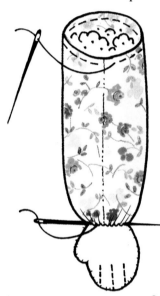

◁ **11** Gather around bottom on edge of fold. Pop hand inside, with 1 in (25 mm) showing. Pull up gathers to fit hand. Stitch through gathers into hand. Fill sleeve enough to hold shape. Gather top ¼ in (6 mm) from edge. Pull up, tucking edge inside.

△ **12** Cut a 4 in (100 mm) length of lace. Gather edge. Pull up. Stitch to wrist. Set aside.

△ **13** Pull up gathers on overskirt to fit exactly halfway around waist. Press well down on top of skirt. Pin. Stitch through gathers into body. Repeat with other piece. Position sleeve on body over the side seam and ½ in (13 mm) down from head. Pin. Take stitches between body and inner side of sleeve top where they touch comfortably. Bend arm at elbow. Pin. Stitch.

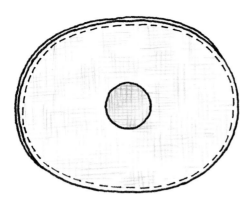

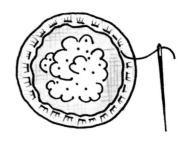

HAT BRIM

△ **14** Cut out centre of one piece only.
Match pieces. Stitch ¼ in (6 mm) from edge.
Trim edge. Turn to right side. Carefully
push out the edges of the seams. Iron.

CROWN

△ **15** Gather around on the edge. Pull up
slightly. Fill centre. Pull up to measure
1½ in (38 mm) across in total.

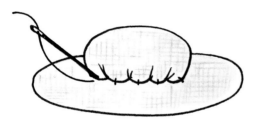

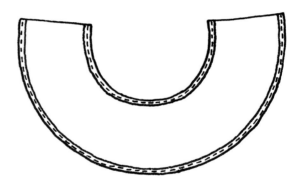

△ **16** Sit crown centrally over hole in brim.
Pin. Stitch between. Don't pull too tight.
The stitches will be hidden by flowers. Set
hat aside.

COLLAR

△ **17** Ease curved edges to wrong side by
⅛ in (3 mm). Pin. Stitch from the right side,
making sure that stitches barely show. Iron.

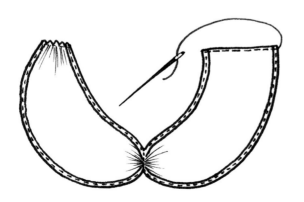

◁ **18** Gather centre back.
Pull up. Gather across both
ends on the very edge. Pull up.

◁ **19** Lay collar over shoulders. Butt front edges together. Stitch between and into body. Stitch centre of collar back to body. Sit hat on top of head, with widest brim at the sides. Pin. Stitch through crown gathers into head. Four big stitches will hold.

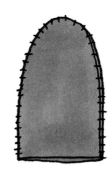

EARS
◁ **20** Trim fur pile very short on all pieces. Match two pieces. Oversew edge. Turn to right side. Iron through a cloth.

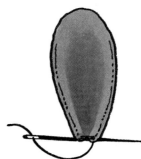

◁ **21** Match bottom corners together. Stitch.

◁ **22** Stretch hat brim flat over head back. Pin. Position ears on the brim at the back so they stand up and face forwards. Press them close to the crown. Stitch through ear bottoms and though brim, catching the head with a couple of stitches. This is quite difficult without making the brim wavy. To keep ears upright, take stitch through the crown into the ears where they touch.

ROSES FOR HAT

◁ **23** Cut 12 strips of single white handkerchief tissue 1½ x 4 in (38 x 100 mm). Take care not to tear the tissue. Colour with a very pale felt pen or thin watercolour paint. Allow to dry.

◁ **24** Fold in half through the length. Begin to roll loosely, keeping folded edge level. It does not matter if you squash the roll. Roll more loosely as you go.

△ **25** Pinch bottom edges and twist tight. Ease out rose top with the point of a needle if it is squashed.

◁ **26** Dot glue to the bottom of the roses one at a time and position around hat, pushing into the crown/brim stitches. Cut small leaves from green paper. Glue leaves between roses. Make three small roses for the collar by cutting off the top of finished roses to leave them ⅜ in (10 mm) high. Dot with glue. Carefully press roses over centre front of collar.

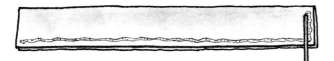

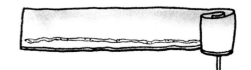

ROSES ON STEM

△ **27** Cut 3 in (75 mm) lengths of thick florist's wire. Cut, colour and fold tissue as before. Smear a small amount of glue across the bottom and down one short edge. Lay one wire over the glue.

△ **28** Roll loosely as before.

◁ **29** Twist the bottom glued edge to the wire. Cut leaves as for hat. Glue to wire behind rose.

◁ **30** Cut a narrow strip of green paper. Glue one end behind rose. Allow glue to dry. Twist tightly around wire. Glue bottom end.

LEAVES FOR BASKET

◁ **31** Cut a few leaves. Twist ends together, three at a time.

▷ **32** Dot glue on twisted ends of leaves. Position in basket. Glue ends of rose stems. Arrange between leaves. Keep roses to one side of the handle to leave room for the arm. Position basket over arm.

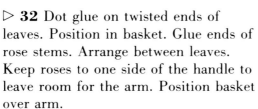

Bertie
·BADGER·

Bertie BADGER

Before starting work read General Instructions on pages 8, 9 and 10.

Materials

Head and ears White and black fur; see General Instruction 2 on page 8.

Eyes Black beads ³⁄₃₂ in (4 mm) in diameter.

Nose, hands and arms Black felt.

Body and legs White felt.

Shoes Dark brown felt. Stiff card.

Shirt front Check cotton (old shirt).

Pullover Machine-knitted fine wool (cut from an old cardigan). Fine crewel wool in two colours (for stitched pattern).

Bow tie Red spotted cotton.

Coat and trousers Rough speckled tweed (old jacket from charity shop). Buttons ³⁄₈ in (10 mm) in diameter.

Pipe Two twigs ³⁄₈ in (10 mm) and ¹⁄₈ in (3 mm) in diameter. Brown felt pen. Clear nail varnish.

Other materials Polyester fibre toy filling. Strong thread. All-purpose clear adhesive.

Patterns

Trace and cut out, keeping to the inside of the line.

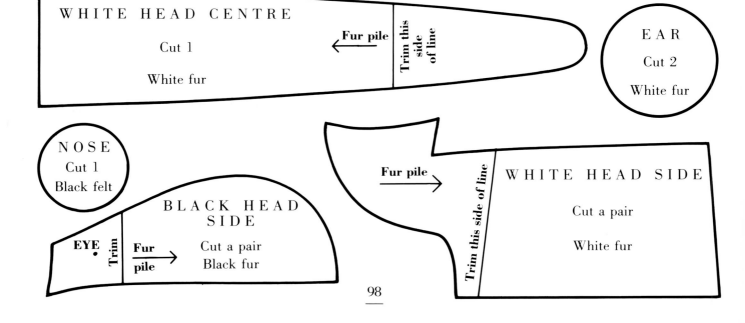

WHITE HEAD CENTRE

Cut 1

White fur

← Fur pile

Trim this side of line

EAR

Cut 2

White fur

NOSE
Cut 1
Black felt

BLACK HEAD SIDE

Cut a pair
Black fur

EYE •

Trim

Fur pile →

Fur pile →

Trim this side of line

WHITE HEAD SIDE

Cut a pair

White fur

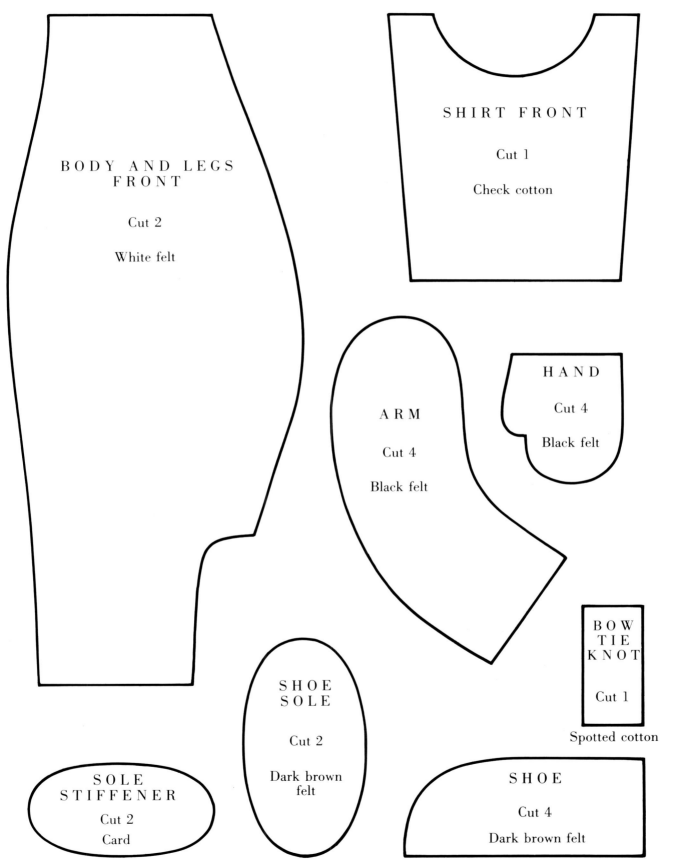

BODY AND LEGS
FRONT

Cut 2

White felt

SHIRT FRONT

Cut 1

Check cotton

ARM

Cut 4

Black felt

HAND

Cut 4

Black felt

BOW
TIE
KNOT

Cut 1

Spotted cotton

SHOE
SOLE

Cut 2

Dark brown
felt

SOLE
STIFFENER

Cut 2

Card

SHOE

Cut 4

Dark brown felt

BERTIE BADGER

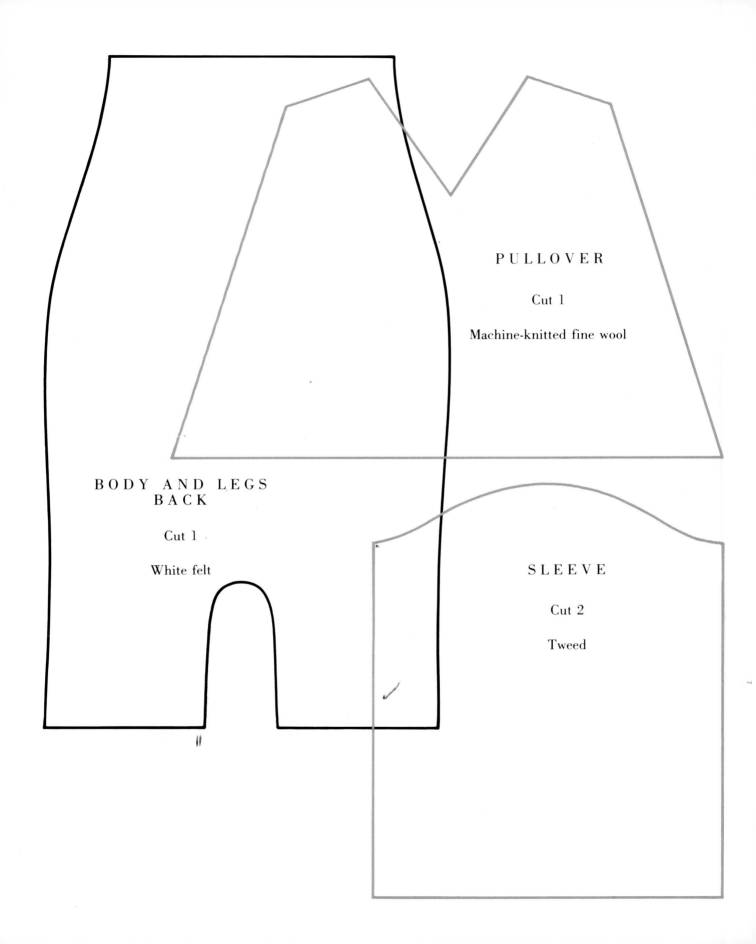

PULLOVER

Cut 1

Machine-knitted fine wool

BODY AND LEGS
BACK

Cut 1

White felt

SLEEVE

Cut 2

Tweed

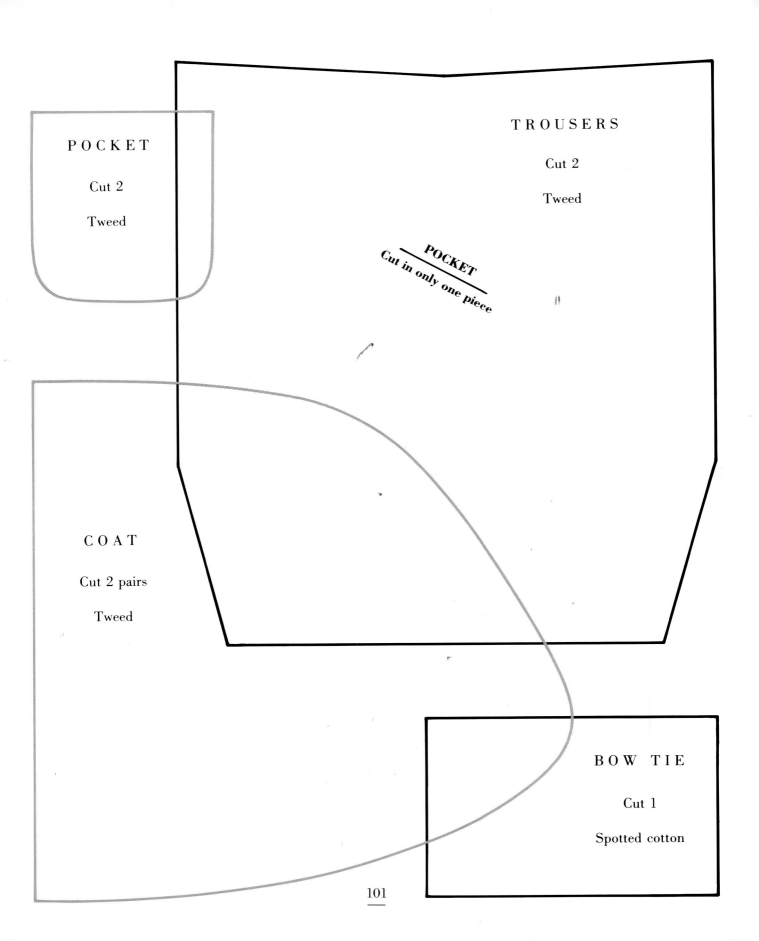

POCKET

Cut 2

Tweed

TROUSERS

Cut 2

Tweed

POCKET
Cut in only one piece

COAT

Cut 2 pairs

Tweed

BOW TIE

Cut 1

Spotted cotton

Bertie BADGER

Instructions

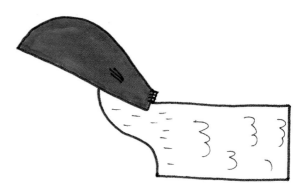

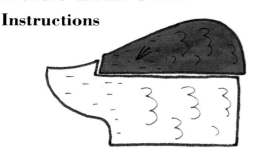

△ **1** Trim fur pile on all head side pieces as shown on pattern. Mark eye positions on both black pieces. Take one black and one white head side. Lay fur side facing up to look like this. These pieces will be stitched together around the L-shaped line between them.

△ **2** Turn the black piece over to match its short edge to the short edge of the white piece, with right sides together. Match top corners of both. Allow the bottom corner of the black to overhang the white piece slightly. Oversew the edge.

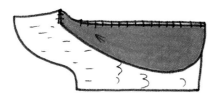

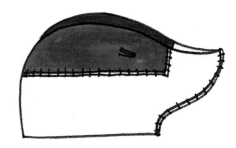

△ **3** Fold to match the long edges with right sides together. Force the corner to fit. Oversew edge, taking extra care in the corner. Open out. Repeat this process with the other head side pieces, not forgetting that they are the opposite way around.

△ **4** Match made-up head sides together. Pin. Oversew front edge.

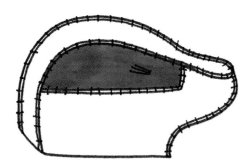

△ **5** Trim pile on head centre piece as marked on pattern. Match centrally into head, with right sides together. Ease edges to fit. Pin. Beginning at the nose, oversew outwards along edges. Turn to right side.

△ **6** Fill head enough to shape well. Gather around on edge. Pull up tight to close.

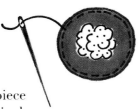

NOSE

▷ **7** Gather around piece on the edge. Roll a pinch of filling into a ball and place in the centre. Pull up gathers tight. Squash into an oval shape. Set aside.

EARS

△ **8** Trim fur pile short on both pieces. Take one piece. Fold in half with wrong sides together. Oversew edge, pulling tight to curve edge. Repeat if necessary.

◁ **9** Position eyes. Check they are 1⅛ in (29 mm) apart. Stitch. Position ears centrally on the black panels, 1¼ in (32 mm) back from the eyes. Stitch. Position nose on the face. Stitch. Set aside.

BODY AND LEGS

10 See instructions for Kenny Koala, steps 10–12, page 67, but note that Bertie Badger is taller and his tummy is smaller.

SHOES

11 See instructions for Freddie Fox, steps 10–12, page 18.

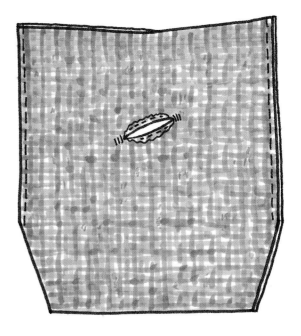

TROUSERS

△ **12** Mark pocket slit on only one trouser piece. Cut on the line. Fold edges of the slit to wrong side by the least amount necessary. Stitch on the edge with close stitches going around a few times to secure from fraying. Make a few tight stitches at each end.

△ **13** Match trouser pieces. Stitch ¼ in (6 mm) from edge.

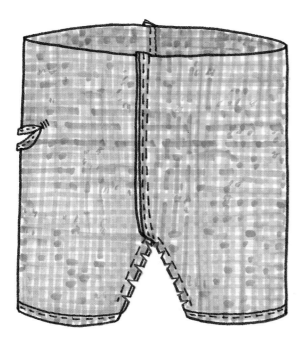

◁ **14** Fold to match inside legs. Stitch. Clip into the seam edges between legs. Fold the edges of the centre seam to one side. Stitch through all layers. Fold up bottom edge by ¼ in (6 mm). Stitch. Turn to right side.

▷ **15** Dress body in trousers. The pocket can be on either side, but it must slope with the high point to the front. Push trouser legs up out of the way. Pin. Press leg bottom over gathers on shoe top, with shoes pointing slightly outwards. Pin. Stitch around twice, pulling together. Pull trousers well up. Slip small pinches of filling low down into the trousers at the back to round the bottom. Fill the trouser front smoothly, spreading filling from side to side to round the tummy. Gather around top. Pull up gathers to fit body. Stitch top to body. Sit head on body. Beginning with large, loose stitches in the centre of both, pull head to body comfortably. Stitch between where they touch. Position shirt front on chest, high under chin. Stitch through edges into body.

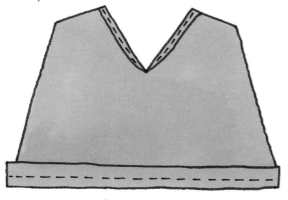

PULLOVER
◁ **16** Fold up bottom edge by ½ in (13 mm). Stitch. Fold V-neck ¼ in (6 mm) to wrong side. The point of the V will be less sharp. Stitch.

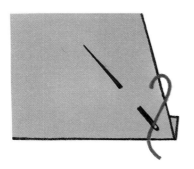 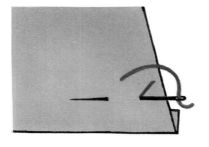 

△ **17** The next step is quite difficult to do neatly. Practise first on some scrap fabric. Stitch a zigzag pattern using one strand of fine crewel wool, making stitches approximately ¼ in (6 mm) long. Do not pull the stitches tight, but allow them to rest on the surface.

△ **18** Stitch five zigzag rows of alternating light and dark wool. Stitch three straight rows around the V-neck. Iron gently through a cloth. Set aside.

BOW TIE
△ **19** With right side outwards, fold long edges to meet. Iron.

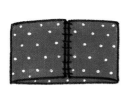

△ **20** Fold short edges to meet. Stitch between.

△ **21** Gather along the stitched centre through all layers. Pull up tight.

KNOT
△ **22** With right sides of knot piece outwards, fold long edges to meet. Iron.

23 Wrap knot around centre. Stitch. Set aside.

COAT
24 See instructions for Brewster Bear, steps 26–30, page 48.

HANDS, ARMS AND SLEEVES
25 See instructions for Freddie Fox, steps 38–44, pages 24–25.

◁ **26** Put pullover on chest, taking care not to stretch it. Pin. Stitch sides and top edges to body. Put a spot of glue behind the bow tie knot. Position on shirt front, high under chin. Fold coat collar ¾ in (19 mm) over to right side. Iron through a cloth. Stitch buttons to coat front. Wrap coat around badger's back with collar high at the back. Pin to body at the front. Assess the position of the sleeve tops. Take a couple of stitches through the coat and into the body at this point.

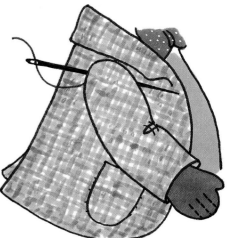

△ **27** Position sleeves on coat side, slanting them slightly forwards. Pin. Take stitches between coat and inner side of sleeve top where they touch comfortably.

PIPE
▷ **28** Make the pipe bowl from a twig ⅜ in (10 mm) in diameter, cutting a piece ½ in (13 mm) long with a fine hacksaw. Sandpaper ends. Taking great care of fingers, push the point of a craft knife into the centre. Turn gradually to take out the centre to a depth of ⅛ in (3 mm). Colour the inside and underneath with a brown felt pen.

▷ **29** Cut the pipe stem from a straight twig and with a diameter of ⅛ in (3 mm) 1½ in (38 mm) long. Sharpen one end to a point, the other into a chisel shape. Gouge a small hole in the side of the bowl by twisting in the knife point. Glue the stem into the bowl. Paint the pipe with a thin layer of clear nail varnish. Glue badger's thumb and first finger to the bowl of the pipe. Tuck the other hand into the pocket. Hold with a stitch.

The Mouse
·FAMILY·

Mrs Maisie MOUSE

Before starting work read General Instructions on pages 8, 9 and 10.

Materials

Head Brown fur; see General Instruction 2, page 8.

Eyes Black beads $\frac{5}{32}$ in (4 mm) in diameter.

Ears, nose, hands and tail Brown felt to match fur.

Body and legs White felt.

Shoes Black felt. Stiff card.

Bloomers, apron, collar and underskirt White cotton.

Dress Pink gingham (if gingham is fine, also cut pieces from white cotton to give more substance to the dress).

Hat Natural-coloured linen (skirt from charity shop). Pink ribbon $\frac{1}{4}$ in (6 mm) wide. Lace daisy (cut from length of guipure lace). Yellow felt pen. Polyester fibre toy filling. All-purpose adhesive. Strong thread. Threads to match felt.

Patterns

Trace and cut out, keeping to the inside of the line.

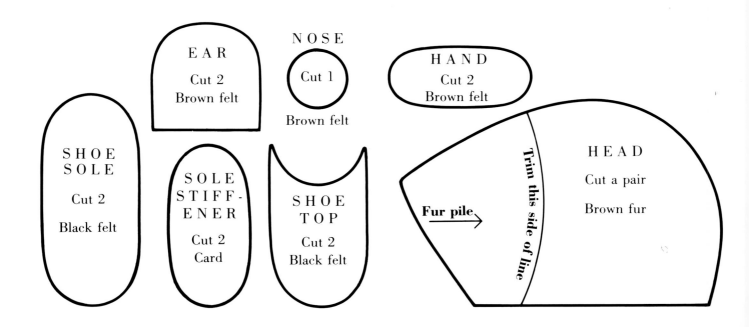

EAR
Cut 2
Brown felt

NOSE
Cut 1
Brown felt

HAND
Cut 2
Brown felt

SHOE SOLE
Cut 2
Black felt

SOLE STIFFENER
Cut 2
Card

SHOE TOP
Cut 2
Black felt

HEAD
Cut a pair
Brown fur

Fur pile →

Trim this side of line

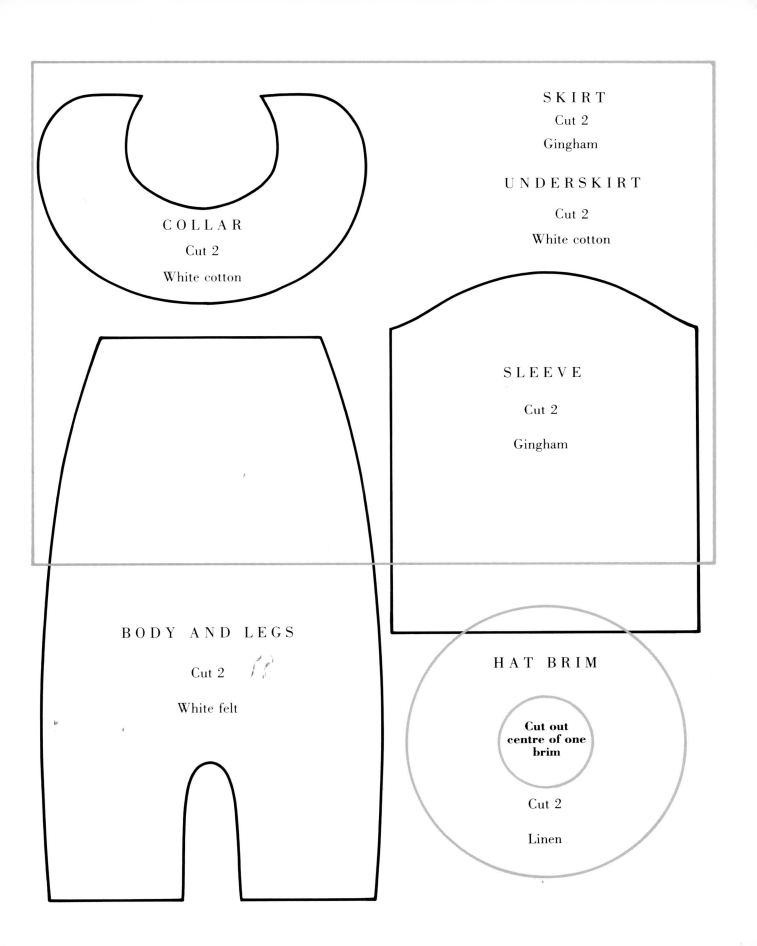

COLLAR

Cut 2

White cotton

SKIRT

Cut 2

Gingham

UNDERSKIRT

Cut 2

White cotton

SLEEVE

Cut 2

Gingham

BODY AND LEGS

Cut 2

White felt

HAT BRIM

Cut out
centre of one
brim

Cut 2

Linen

HAT CROWN

Cut 1

Linen

BLOOMERS

Cut 2

White cotton

APRON
BOW

Cut 1

White
cotton

APRON
POCKET

Cut 1

White cotton

APRON
STRING

Cut 1

White cotton

TAIL   Cut 1   Brown felt

DRESS
BODICE

Cut 2

Gingham

APRON

Cut 1

White
cotton

Mrs Maisie MOUSE

Instructions

HEAD

△ **1** Trim fur pile on both pieces as shown on pattern.

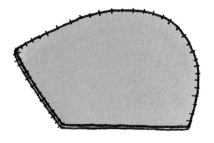

△ **2** Match head pieces. Oversew edge, taking extra care around nose point. Turn to right side.

△ **3** Fill head firmly, keeping nose pointed and back well rounded. Gather around bottom on the edge. Pull up tight to close.

NOSE

△ **4** Gather on edge. Pull up tight to close. Stitch back and forth over gathers, pulling tight until nose measures ¼ in (6 mm) across.

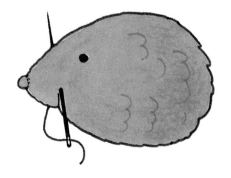

◁ **5** Position nose on the front point of face. Stitch. Using strong thread, take a stitch from side to side ½ in (13 mm) back from nose, allowing the thread to loop underneath. Pull tight to indent face. Repeat a couple of times. Position bead eyes with their centres 1 in (25 mm) apart and the same distance from nose. Stitch.

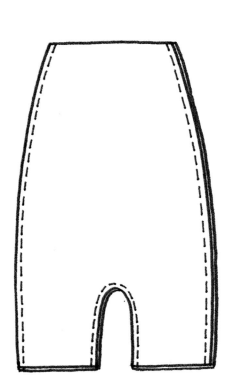 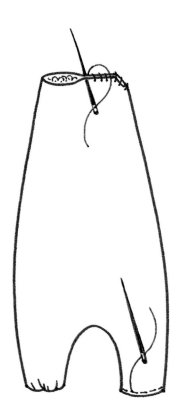

BODY AND LEGS

△ **6** Match pieces. Stitch ¼ in (6 mm) from the edge. Trim edges close to stitching. Turn to right side.

△ **7** Fill firmly up to openings. Take care not to stretch the felt upwards while filling. Gather around leg bottoms on the edge. Pull up tight to close. Match open top edges together. Pin. Oversew on edge, tucking corner points inside. Set aside.

SHOES

△ **8** Match one top to one sole. Oversew edge. Turn to right side.

△ **9** Slip card stiffener well into shoe. Fill shoe between top and card. Gather around on the edge.

△ **10** Pull up tight to close. Set aside.

DRESS BODICE

△ **11** Match pieces. Stitch ¼ in (6 mm) from edge. Trim edge. Turn to right side. *Gingham fabrics can be flimsy, and if your material is fine, cut all pieces from white cotton as well and make up double with the gingham. (All drawings and instructions are shown as gingham only.)*

△ **12** Gather around bottom. Pull bodice over body, matching side seams. Pull up to fit, although the whole bodice will be slightly loose. Stitch through gathers into body.

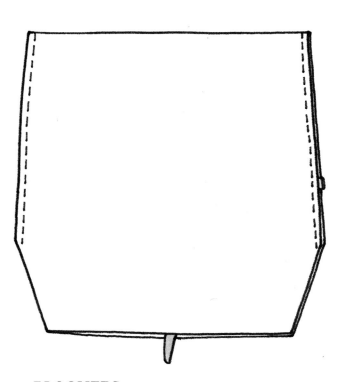

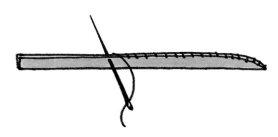

TAIL

△ **13** Fold tail to match long edges. Oversew carefully on the very edge with tiny, close stitches. Push a thin wooden dowel or metal knitting needle into the tail so that it stays round while you gently iron over the stitching through a cloth.

BLOOMERS

△ **14** Match pieces with tail sandwiched between and end showing 2½ in (63 mm) down from top. Pin. Stitch ¼ in (6 mm) from edge, including tail end in stitches.

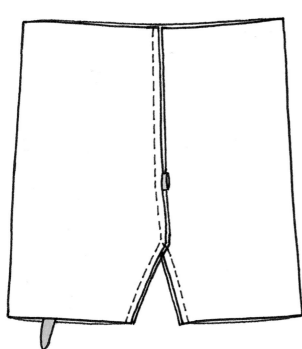

△ **15** Fold to match inside legs. Stitch. Trim inside leg seam edges. Turn to right side.

△ **16** Dress body in bloomers. Push bloomer legs up out of the way. Pin. Press leg bottom over gathers on shoe top, with toes pointing slightly outwards. Pin. Stitch around, pulling together. Slip small pinches of filling into the bloomers around the legs and body, with a little more in the back to round the bottom. Gather top ¼ in (6 mm) from the edge. Fold inside on the gathers. Pull up to fit. Stitch through the top into body. Gather around bottom of bloomer leg ¼ in (6 mm) from the edge. Fold inside on gathers. Pull up to fit. Hold to shoe top with a stitch. Sit head on body. Beginning with large, loose stitches in the centre of both, pull head to body comfortably. Stitch between where they touch.

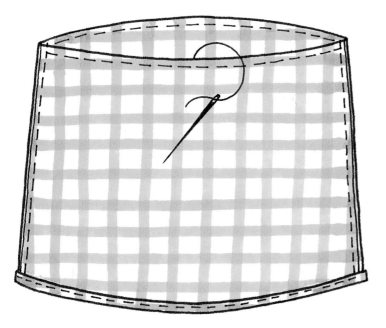

UNDERSKIRT AND SKIRT

△ **17** Use the white cotton lining as an underskirt. Cut it ½ in (13 mm) shorter than the skirt. Make separately and put on body following skirt instructions. Match skirt pieces. Stitch sides ¼ in (6 mm) from edge. Fold up bottom edge by ¼ in (6 mm). Stitch. Gather around top, ¼ in (6 mm) from edge. Leaving thread attached, turn to right side. Set aside.

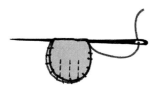

HANDS

△ **18** Take one piece. Fold in half. Oversew edge. Stitch three equal lines through both layers. Take a needle side to side through the fold. Pull up slightly.

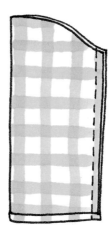

SLEEVES

△ **19** Fold up bottom edge by ¼ in (6 mm). Iron. Fold matching edges. Stitch ¼ in (6 mm) from edge. Turn to right side.

△ **20** Gather around bottom edge of fold. Pull up tight. Butt hand to gathers on sleeve. Stitch between. Fill sleeve enough to hold shape. Gather top ¼ in (6 mm) from edge. Pull up, tucking edges inside.

△ **21** Dress body in skirt. Fold top inside on gathers. Pull up to fit, pressing well down over bloomers and underskirt. Stitch through top into body. Position sleeve on body side ½ in (13 mm) down from head and sloping slightly forwards. Pin. Take stitches between body and inner side of sleeve top, where they touch comfortably. Bend arm. Pin. Stitch across fold.

APRON POCKET

▷ **22** Fold all edges ¼ in (6 mm) to wrong side. Iron.

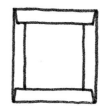

APRON

◁ **23** Fold three edges ¼ in (6 mm) to wrong side. Iron. Stitch invisibly. Position pocket. Stitch. Gather across apron top ⅛ in (3 mm) from edge. Pull up to measure 2 in (50 mm) across the top. See instructions for Bertha Bear's apron tie, steps 23 and 24, page 58, but note that Maisie Mouse has no lace on her apron. Wrap apron around body touching skirt top. Stitch ties at back.

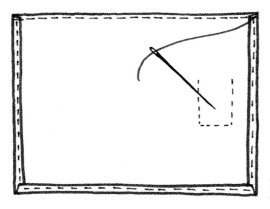

APRON BOW

24 Fold long edges to meet in the centre. Iron. See instructions for Bertha Bear's bow, step 28, page 59. Glue bow over apron ties at centre back.

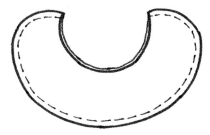

COLLAR

△ **25** Match pieces. Stitch ¼ in (6 mm) from edge. Trim away edge close to stitching. Turn to right side. Iron. Set aside.

HAT

26 See instructions for Rosie Rabbit's hat, steps 14–16, page 93, but note that Maisie Mouse's hat has a smaller, round brim and the crown measure 1¼ in (32 mm) across.

EARS

▷ **28** Take one piece. Fold to match corners. Oversew edge.

BOW

◁ **30** Cut a piece of ribbon 4 in (100 mm) long. Fold into a bow shape, threading centres onto a needle. Stitch. Glue to hat back.

△ **27** Sit hat on top of head. Pin. Stitch through crown gathers into head. Four big stitches will hold. Lay collar around neck, tucked under head. Stitch centre fronts to body.

△ **29** Position ears on brim so they face forwards and line up with the back edge of the crown. Stitch bottom of ears to brim. Take a stitch through one ear bottom and crown, through the head into the other ear bottom and back again. Cut a piece of ribbon to fit around the crown. Glue into place.

HAT FLOWER

◁ **31** Colour the centre of one lace daisy with a yellow felt pen. Glue to front of hatband.

Baby MOUSE

Materials
Head, hands and feet Light brown felt.
Body White felt.
Tail Fine string. Brown felt pen.
Other materials Polyester fibre toy filling. Black
embroidery thread. Thread to match felt.

Patterns
Trace and cut out, keeping to the inside of the
line.

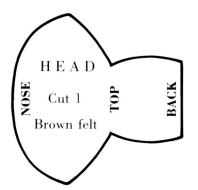

HEAD
NOSE
Cut 1
TOP
BACK
Brown felt

BODY AND LEGS

Cut 2

White felt

EAR
Brown
felt
Cut 2

Cut 2
Brown
felt

HAND

Cut 2
Brown
felt

FOOT

Instructions

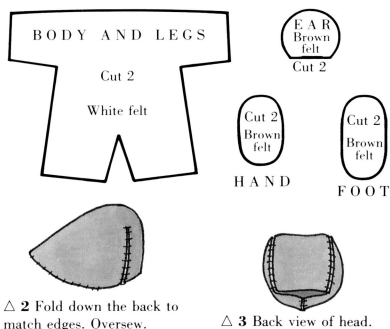

HEAD
△ **1** Fold head piece in
half. Oversew front edges
with tiny, tight stitches.
Stop ¼ in (6 mm) before
the bottom corner.

△ **2** Fold down the back to
match edges. Oversew.

▷ **4** Turn head to right
side. Fill up to the opening.
Gather around opening on
the edge. Pull up tight,
tucking edges inside.

△ **3** Back view of head.

TAIL
5 Cut a piece of string 2 in (50 mm) long. Colour with
brown felt pen. Dry.

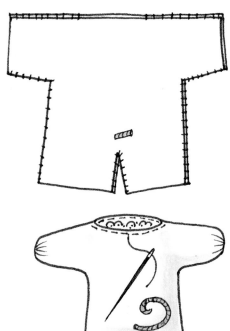

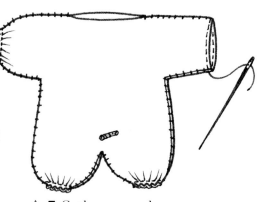

BODY AND LEGS

◁ **6** Snip a tiny hole in one body piece, centrally and 1⅛ in (29 mm) from the top. Thread end of string through the hole and hold with a stitch between felt and string. Match body pieces, with the tail inside. Oversew edge, leaving arm and leg ends and ¾ in (19 mm) of centre top open.

△ **7** Gather around arms and legs on the very edge. Pull up tight to close.

△ **8** Carefully turn body to right side. Fill softly with small pinches of filling in the arms and legs. Fill tummy until rounded. Gather around top on the edge. Pull up tight to close.

EARS

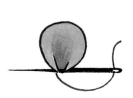

△ **9** Take one piece and pinch bottom corners together. Stitch.

△ **10** Sit head on body. Stitch between where they meet comfortably. Take a stitch from side to side ¼ in (6 mm) back from nose, allowing the thread to loop underneath. Pull tight to indent the face. Make tiny eyes with close stitches in black thread ⅜ in (10 mm) apart and back from nose. Position ears on top of head, with centres ½ in (13 mm) apart. Stitch.

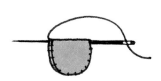

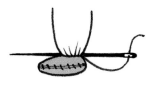

HANDS

△ **11** Take one piece and fold it in half. Oversew edge. Take needle side to side through the fold. Pull up slightly.

△ **12** Butt hand to arm. Stitch between.

FEET

△ **13** Repeat as hands. Butt to leg, with foot pointed forwards. Stitch.

14 For baby to suck his thumb, take a stitch from the mouth to the hand and back again, then through the neck to the back to fasten off. Position baby in mother's arms. Stitch baby's body to mother's bodice and mother's hand to baby's body.

Miss Molly MOUSE

Before starting work read General Instructions on pages 8, 9 and 10.

Materials

Head Brown fur; see General Instruction 2, page 8.

Eyes Black beads ⁵⁄₃₂ in (4 mm) in diameter.

Ears, nose, hands and tail Brown felt to match fur.

Body and legs White felt.

Shoes Black felt. Stiff card.

Bloomers White cotton.

Dress Printed cotton. Broderie anglaise lace ⁵⁄₈ in (16 mm) wide.

Skipping-rope Two wooden beads, no larger than ½ in (13 mm) in diameter. Two matchsticks. Felt pen the same colour as beads. Stiff string.

Other materials Polyester fibre toy filling. All-purpose clear adhesive. Strong thread. Thread to match felt.

Patterns

Trace and cut out, keeping to the inside of the line.

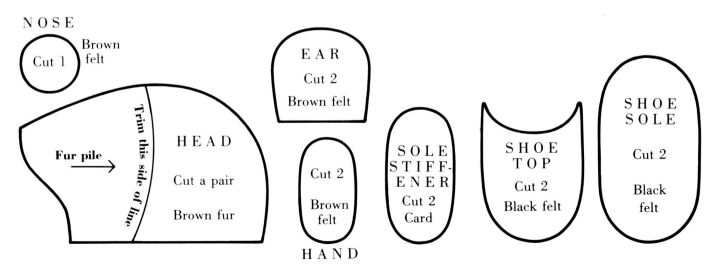

NOSE
Cut 1 Brown felt

HEAD
Cut a pair
Brown fur

Fur pile →

Trim this side of line

EAR
Cut 2
Brown felt

HAND
Cut 2
Brown felt

SOLE STIFF-ENER
Cut 2
Card

SHOE TOP
Cut 2
Black felt

SHOE SOLE
Cut 2
Black felt

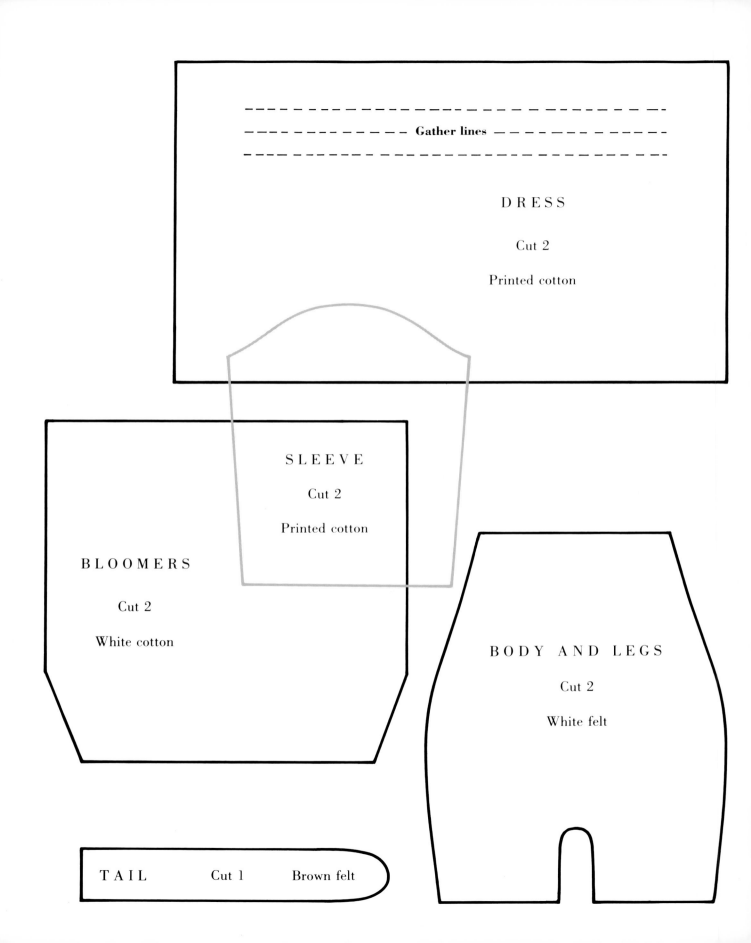

Gather lines

DRESS

Cut 2

Printed cotton

SLEEVE

Cut 2

Printed cotton

BLOOMERS

Cut 2

White cotton

BODY AND LEGS

Cut 2

White felt

TAIL   Cut 1   Brown felt

Miss Molly MOUSE

Instructions

HEAD AND NOSE

1 See instructions for Maisie Mouse, steps 1–4, page 111.

EARS

◁ **2** Take one piece. Fold to match corners. Oversew.

BODY, LEGS AND SHOES

4 See instructions for Maisie Mouse, steps 6–10, page 112.

TAIL AND BLOOMERS

5 See instructions for Maisie Mouse, steps 13–15, pages 113–14. Sandwich tail in the back seam, 1¾ in (45 mm) from the top.

◁ **3** Position nose on the front point of the face. Stitch. Using strong thread, take a stitch side to side ½ in (13 mm) back from nose, allowing the thread to loop underneath. Pull tight to indent face. Repeat a couple of times. Position bead eyes with centres ¾ in (19 mm) apart and the same distance from the nose. Position ears ¾ in (19 mm) back from eyes, facing forwards with their centres 1 in (25 mm) apart. Pin. Stitch.

◁ **6** Dress body in bloomers. Push bloomer legs up out of the way. Pin. Press bottom of leg over gathers on shoe top, with toes pointing slightly outwards. Pin. Stitch around, pulling together. Slip small pinches of filling into the bloomers around the leg tops and body, with a little more in the back to round the bottom. Gather top ¼ in (6 mm) from the edge. Fold inside on the gathers. Pull up gathers to fit. Stitch through the top into the body. Gather around bottom of bloomer leg ¼ in (6 mm) from the edge. Fold inside on the gathers. Pull up gathers to fit. Hold to shoe top with a stitch. Sit head on body. Beginning with large, loose stitches in the centre of both, pull head to body comfortably. Stitch between where they touch.

DRESS

▷ **7** Draw gather lines on the wrong side of both pieces with a sharp pencil and ruler. Gather on lines with tiny stitches, leaving ends of threads 6 in (150 mm) long and all coming out of the right side of the fabric. Fold up bottom edge by ¼ in (6 mm) to wrong side. Iron.

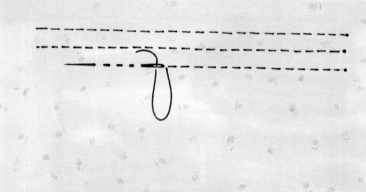

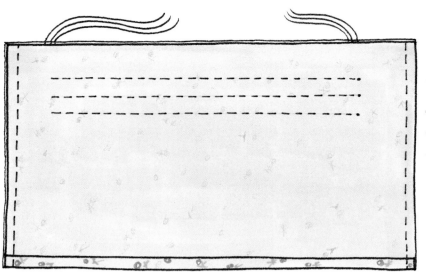

◁ **8** Match dress pieces with right sides together. Stitch ¼ in (6 mm) from edge. Turn to right side. Open seams out flat. Iron.

▽ **9** Wrap loose threads around a pin. Match lace to bottom edge with only a little showing. Pin. Fold short ends of lace over and butt the folds. Stitch. Gather around top on the edge.

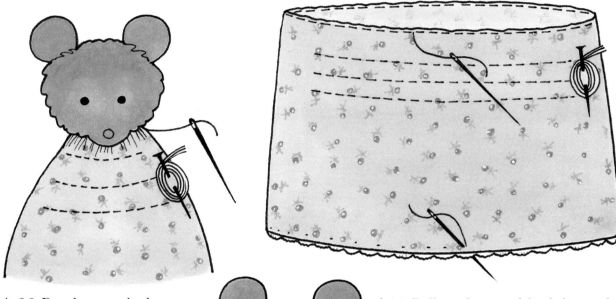

△ **10** Put dress on body, lining up side seams. Pin over side seams. Pull up top gathers to fit tight under the head. Spread gathers evenly. Fasten off thread.

◁ **11** Pull up front and back lines of gathers to fit the body. Adjust the evenness with the point of a needle. Fasten off each of the six gather threads individually, by stitching into the body.

HANDS AND SLEEVES
12 See instructions for Maisie Mouse, steps 18–20, page 115.

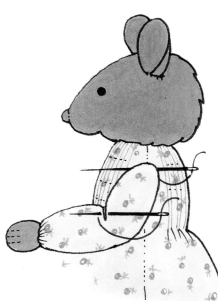

◁ **13** Position sleeve on side of body, ¼ in (6 mm) down from head and sloping slightly forwards. Pin. Take stitches between body and inner side of sleeve top where they touch comfortably. Bend arm. Pin. Stitch across fold.

△ **14** Cut a 7 in (175 mm) length of lace. Trim away raw edge to leave lace ½ in (13 mm) wide. Fold over ends. Gather across on the edge.

△ **15** Pull up gathers to fit around neck tight under the head. Stitch across folded ends.

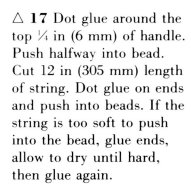

SKIPPING-ROPE

△ **16** Cut two pieces of matchstick 1⅛ in (29 mm) long. Smoothly sharpen one end by rubbing on sandpaper. Colour with felt pen to match beads.

△ **17** Dot glue around the top ¼ in (6 mm) of handle. Push halfway into bead. Cut 12 in (305 mm) length of string. Dot glue on ends and push into beads. If the string is too soft to push into the bead, glue ends, allow to dry until hard, then glue again.

△ **18** Wrap hands around handles. Stitch between finger tips and wrist.

Master Monty MOUSE

Before starting work read General Instructions on pages 8, 9 and 10.

Materials

Head Brown fur; see General Instruction 2, page 8.

Eyes Black beads ⅛₂ in (4 mm) in diameter.

Ears, nose, hands and tail Brown felt to match fur.

Body and legs White felt.

Shoes Black felt. Stiff card.

Trousers Dark blue denim (cut from an old skirt).

Jumper Machine-knitted fine wool (cut from an old jumper that has a rib pattern around the bottom edge).

Other materials Polyester fibre toy filling. Strong thread. Threads to match felt.

Patterns

Trace and cut out, keeping to the inside of the line.

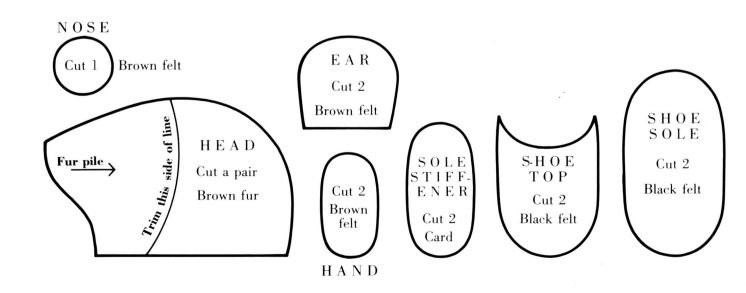

NOSE

Cut 1 Brown felt

EAR
Cut 2
Brown felt

Fur pile →

Trim this side of line

HEAD
Cut a pair
Brown fur

Cut 2
Brown felt

HAND

SOLE STIFF-ENER
Cut 2
Card

SHOE TOP
Cut 2
Black felt

SHOE SOLE
Cut 2
Black felt

TROUSERS

Cut a pair

Dark blue denim

BACK

FRONT

SLEEVE

Cut 2

Knitted wool

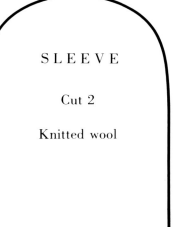

POLO NECK

Cut 1

Rib pattern knitted wool

TAIL   Cut 1   Brown felt

JUMPER BODY

Cut 2

Knitted wool

RIB PATTERN

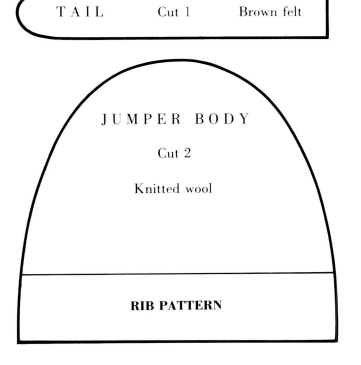

BODY AND LEGS

Cut 2

White felt

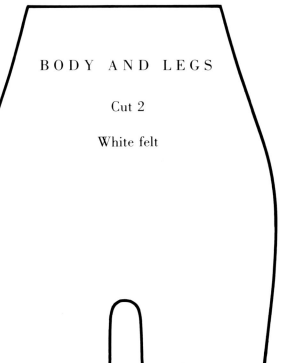

Master Monty MOUSE

Instructions

HEAD AND NOSE

1 See instructions for Maisie Mouse, steps 1–4, page 111.

EARS

◁ **2** Take one piece. Fold to match corners. Oversew.

△ **3** Position nose on the front point of the face. Stitch. Using strong thread, take a stitch from side to side, ½ in (13 mm) back from nose, allowing the thread to loop underneath. Pull tight to indent face. Repeat a couple of times. Position bead eyes with centres ¾ in (19 mm) apart and the same distance from the nose. Position ears ¾ in (19 mm) back from eyes, facing forwards with their centres 1 in (25 mm) apart. Pin. Stitch.

BODY, LEGS AND SHOES

4 See instructions for Maisie Mouse, steps 6–10, page 112.

TAIL

5 See instructions for Maisie Mouse, step 13, page 113. Set aside.

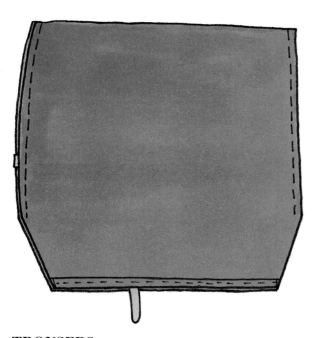

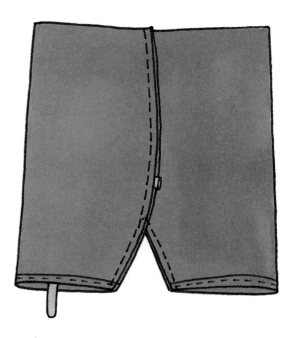

TROUSERS

△ **6** Take one piece. Fold bottom edges up ¼ in (6 mm) to wrong side. Stitch. Repeat with other piece. Match pieces with tail sandwiched in the back seam and end just showing 1¾ in (45 mm) from the trouser

top. Pin. Stitch ¼ in (6 mm) from edge, including tail end in the stitches.

△ **7** Fold to match inside legs. Stitch. Trim inside leg seam edges. Turn to right side.

▷ **8** Dress body in trousers. Push trouser legs up out of the way. Press leg bottom over gathers on shoe top, with toes pointing slightly outwards. Pin. Stitch around, pulling together. Slip small pinches of filling into the trousers around the leg tops and body, with a little more in the back to round the bottom. Gather top ¼ in (6 mm) from edge. Fold inside on the gathers. Pull up gathers to fit. Stitch through top into body.

JUMPER BODY

◁ **9** Cut pieces including ¾ in (19 mm) of rib pattern. Match pieces. Stitch ¼ in (6 mm) from the edge. Trim edge. Fold up bottom ¼ in (6 mm) to wrong side. Stitch invisibly. Turn to right side.

◁ **10** Pull jumper over the body, lining up side seams. Stitch across top into body.

HANDS

11 See instructions for Maisie Mouse, step 18, page 115.

SLEEVES

△ **12** Take one piece. Fold up bottom edge by ¼ in (6 mm). Fold matching edges. Stitch ¼ in (6 mm) from edge, leaving top open. Turn to right side.

△ **13** Gather around bottom of sleeve on the edge of fold. Pull up tight. Butt hand to gathers. Stitch between. Fill sleeve enough to hold shape, but do not stretch. Gather around top ¼ in (6 mm) from edge. Pull up, tucking edges inside.

◁ **14** Sit head on body, tilting slightly forwards. Beginning with large, loose stitches in the centre of both, pull head to body comfortably. Stitch between where they touch. Position sleeve on side of body ½ in (13 mm) down from head. Pin. Take stitches between body and inner side of the sleeve top, where they touch comfortably. Bend arm. Pin. Stitch across fold.

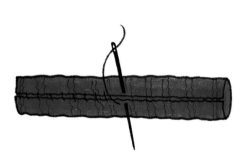

POLO NECK
△ **15** Cut from rib pattern. Fold long edges to meet. Stitch between edges.

△ **16** Wrap polo around neck. Butt edges at the back. Pin. Stitch between.